Persistence of Light

Persistence of Light

in a Japanese Prison Camp,
with an Elephant Crossing the Alps,
and then in Silicon Valley

John Hoyte

Best wishes

John Hoyte

Terra Nova Books
Santa Fe, New Mexico

Library of Congress Control Number 2018941046

Distributed by SCB Distributors, (800) 729-6423

Terra Nova Books

Published by Terra Nova Books, Santa Fe, New Mexico.
www.TerraNovaBooks.com

ISBN 978-1-948749-06-0

Your memory is made of light.
—Pablo Neruda

We do not remember days, we remember moments.
—Cesare Pavese

This is a story for my grandchildren but also for a wider readership, to show through my adventures the wonder and mystery of life. It is set to Isaac Newton's seven colors of the rainbow. They provide a framework for my life story. Each color is unique and beautiful. Together they make white light complete.

Contents

Preface

"Cancel plans for your summer vacation. We are crossing the Alps again, following Hannibal—but this
time with an elephant!"

Such was the letter I received from John Hoyte in January
1959. I was sitting outside my little mud house in Baringo, Kenya,
high in the Great Rift Valley, two hundred miles north of Nairobi,
where the mail was still being brought by runner. Was I dream-
ing? Was this a joke? Had I been too long away from friends in
England?

In fact, I was at that moment with my very senior boss, the
commissioner of community development, who had come up
from Nairobi for me to hand-over at the end of my two-year assignment. In spite of the deference due, letters from England
were special, and I asked if he would mind if I read the letter that
had just been delivered. He agreed. But when I read it, I wondered if I should burst out laughing or what. I decided to share
with him the extraordinary news: an expedition with an elephant
across the Alps next summer! He looked at me as if I had caught
the madness. But it was not madness. It was John Hoyte. John
was always one for somewhat-crazy ideas—surprising, exciting,
and out of the ordinary but each time ending up with challenge,
fun, and friendship.

I had first met John when we were final-year students at
Cambridge University, in adjacent buildings, he in St John's College studying engineering, me just across the river in Magdalene,
studying economics. We were discussing neither engineering nor
economics but history—which route Hannibal had followed

across the Alps in 218 B.C., some 2174 years earlier. A well-watched TV program had just presented a new theory about which route the great general had taken from France to Italy, arguing that Hannibal and his army had crossed by the Col de la Traversette, one of the highest and southernmost passes between France and Italy. The theory presented new evidence about dates and climate change, and seemed convincing. But Dr. A.H. McDonald, the distinguished Cambridge professor of classics, strongly disagreed and demolished the ideas with details from the accounts of Livy and Polybius. McDonald ended his critical review by saying that if anyone really wanted to know, they should cross the Alps and see for themselves.

So far from being dusty and distant, the discussion between John and me was vivid and practical. John was excited. Why don't we explore the Alpine crossings on our coming summer vacation? Easily persuaded by John's enthusiasm, I readily agreed. And a month or two later, there we were—John, me, John's sister, and another, hitchhiking from Switzerland to France and then on to Italy. Being impecunious students, we stayed in youth hostels, taking photographs and exploring how well various passes matched the accounts of Livy and Polybius. We had a fun time, wrote an account of our travels for the London *Times*, (published as "Cambridge Carthaginians") and celebrated by taking ourselves to the opera in Covent Garden. After that, we each got on with the next phase of our lives, John as a budding engineer in Birmingham, myself working in upcountry Kenya in community development.

John, however, didn't let go. Preoccupied with what we had seen and our belief that a different pass, the Col de Clapier, fit the classic accounts much better than the Traversette, he continued his explorations. One summer, he crossed the Pyrenees from Spain to France, an earlier part of Hannibal's epic journey. Then in 1958, shortly before he wrote to me, he had a vision one sleepless night: We should put our theory to the test, this time with an elephant. Another case of John and his wacky ideas!

But beyond our wonderful journey over the Alps, *Persistence of Light* is about so much else too which makes up John's fascinating story: his life and passions, growing up in China, being educated in England, moving to the United States, starting his own business and more. Now in his eighties, he is still full of his commitments and enthusiasms for life. With family and friends, we are celebrating a reunion of the Hannibal crossing by climbing to the Col de Clapier in July 2018.

John's book, like his life, is an inspiration, full of fun, warm friendships, unexpected happenings, and serious achievement. A well-lived life, still on the move. I am sure Jumbo would agree.

Sir Richard Jolly,
Lewes, Sussex, England
March 2018

Acknowledgments

My deepest thanks to Laurel Leigh, Andrew Shattuck McBride, David Greene, and Paul Willis for their wisdom and editorial skills. They guided me in the journey of my writing, from memories of a childhood in China to an Alpine adventure to the overarching theme of the *persistence of light* in my life with all its colors. Like a jigsaw puzzle, the pieces started to fit.

Thanks to Lisa, Ben, Jonathan, and Martina for their helpful input. They gave meaning and purpose to this whole enterprise and provided delightful grandchildren, Rachel, Nicki and Alma, to pass on the story.

Many thanks to Marty Gerber and the team at Terra Nova Books for encouragement and for making this book a reality.

My thanks to Sir Richard Jolly for his deep friendship over the years, his camaraderie on the Hannibal expedition, and for contributing the Preface to this memoir.

Special thanks to David Thelwell for permission to include his father's hilarious cartoon of an elephant dashing off from London Zoo to join our expedition.

My special thanks to my spouse and dear love, Luci Shaw, for her editorial skills, her encouragement, patience, and overall caring for me in all my struggles, frustrations, and joys.

CHAPTER 1

A Childhood in China

Red is the color, red for China, red for violence, red for the heart of a family torn apart. Its wavelength range is 620 to 740 nanometers.

EARLY MEMORIES

My father, Stanley Hoyte, went out to China in the fall of 1913. There he was at age twenty-eight, a young doctor, single, in a strange land and out of touch with the England he had left and the terrors of the impending First World War. But life in China was by no means easy. Just thirteen years earlier, in the Boxer Rebellion, 156 missionaries had been killed in the province of his destination. There were plagues, anti-British riots, and transportation by foot. At that time, he was the only Western-trained surgeon in a province of 5 million people. He had qualified as a surgeon at Middlesex Hospital in London. For his help with a plague prevention campaign, he had received a prestigious medal and decoration from the Chinese government. It is easy to forget the dangers he faced, working in plague-infested villages. He had volunteered to go to China as a medical missionary through a British nonprofit organization called the China Inland Mission. His mission was to bring the message of God's love through the gift of healing. His first stint in the field was hard and lonely. It was considered inappropriate for him to be seen in public talking to anyone of the opposite sex, as this could be considered as propositioning her.

On his way back to England at the end of that first term, he was asked to escort an ailing missionary to the U.S. and so went to Montclair, New Jersey, while in the country, to visit the Wilder family, whom he had met while a medical student in London. Grace, my mother, twenty-four at the time, opened the front door for him, and Dad, so he told us later, fell in love with her right there and then! Three years later, they were married in Beijing (then called Peking) and spent the summer in a mat-shed on a mountaintop west of the mission hospital. I can imagine their intimacy and love-making in those wild mountains of central China.

The hospital where my parents served was in the distant town of Linfen, Shanxi Province, southwest of Beijing, and in those days, it took eight weeks by oxcart and foot to reach it from the coast. I prefer the ancient name Ping Yang Fu, as it reminded me of old Imperial China. It was there, in 1932, that I was born. Two years earlier, Dad had bought an old derelict mill up in the wooded hills some four hours away by horse-drawn *droshky*, renovated it, and built a round moon gate between the stables and the main living area, a paddling pool, prayer tower, and a little bridge over the stream. This became our cool, summer home. The temperature in Linfen could be well over a hundred degrees. Memories of the old mill in the cool hills above the hot and dusty town were to be for the rest of my life a source of peace and security, family love and playfulness.

My toes made delicate ripples on the surface.

One of my first memories is of light and love. The vividness of that experience has helped me make light the overarching theme for this memoir and reflected something of my mother's strong, all-encircling love. At first I was the youngest of five children, then became one of six when baby Elizabeth was born, and yet there seemed to be an almost infinite capacity for my mother to love each of us to the very depth of her being.

The moment is with me now. She is holding me over the mill stream. She is standing on the little bridge and my toes are just touching the flowing, crystal-clear water, making delicate and to me delightful ripples on the surface. Light on the water. It was magic! Perhaps this was my introduction to art, for my mother was a talented artist, and her sketches and little water colors decorated her letters during those lean, devastating years of separation while we were in the Japanese prison camp.

Another early memory was of the huge beam in the main room of the mill and how my older brothers and sister were able to climb up onto it by rope ladder while I couldn't. I wanted to so badly! Having four older siblings—particularly Mary, the nearest in age—who would be willing to climb anything no matter how seemingly dangerous, I was always trying to catch up.

I also remember finding a spent bullet in the garden. Dad had it made into a clasp for me, one I still keep as a memento of our summer home. How it survived the boarding school and Weihsien prison camp I do not know, but that bullet reminds me of two aspects of our childhood in China—one, the love and caring my father had for me, that he should bother to make a discovery into a keepsake, and the other the constant threat of physical danger that we as a family and other foreigners faced. Our parents wisely protected us from the stark reality of this, and demonstrated undaunted courage when danger was near.

Years later, while taking an introductory class on journal keeping, I was asked to write a brief description of my father's face. In a flash the memory came back to me of kissing his rough, half-

Robin, Eric, Rupert, Mary, me and Elizabeth.

shaven cheek "Good night."That may well have been my first
memory. Most things around me, as a two-year-old, were soft
and cuddly, but here was my Dad, strong and, to me, all powerful. The roughness of his skin came as a wild and wonderful
shock. The tactile nature of another world indicated a rough edge
to things, an unexpected surprise and so an adventure.

The year before I was born, Dad bought an old Trojan car with
a crank handle at the front to start it. Getting back and forth to
the mill was quite an adventure. In 1933, for instance, Dad's diary
notes, the heavy rains made roads impassible for the car. There
were times when he would drive out of the ruts and across fields
in order to get through.

THE TERRORIST ATTACK

I was two and a half when we moved back from a stay on the
coast to Linfen, although the Chinese civil war was going on and
the town was besieged by Communist forces. They were acting
more like a militarized gang of terrorists, thugs or bandits than
a regular army with central control. They destroyed villages,
killing the landowners and imprisoning the women and children
until their husbands could come up with ransom money. The
year before, the "Reds"had murdered two young American mis-

sionaries, John and Betty Stam. Their three-year-old daughter, Helen, was saved only because a Chinese Christian offered his life for hers and was killed instead. The same brutal section of the Red army crossed the Yellow River and were pillaging our province and threatening to attack Linfen. Mom and Dad must have wondered if we children would be spared if they were killed. My three brothers were safe at Chefoo, but my parents had Mary, age five, me, and one-year-old Elizabeth with them, and my mother's diary recounts the danger.

Was I afraid? I was not afraid of actually dying at their hands. But I was afraid for the children. I should have liked to protect them from being scared or hurt. And yet as I faced this fear, I knew that if I set the right standard, they would be as brave as I wanted them to be. Children are heroes at heart, for all heroic stories appeal greatly to them. So I trusted God to give me courage and strength when the time came to show them how to be brave. . . .

Then came another question. What if we were killed and the children left? I had a talk with good old Mrs. Tang, our children's nurse, who said of course she would do her best for them in that case, and let me say here, what a help it is in such straits to face each question honestly and to talk it out with the person concerned. It is wonderful what strength God gives in our desperate situation.

Then came another question. What about our three boys at boarding school on the coast? We faced it together. It would seem terrible to deprive them of a mother's and a father's loving sympathy and continued care. It was a great relief to write to Robin a long letter

telling him of the facts and of what might happen to us,
saying how brave we knew he and his brothers would
have been if they were here and urging them to keep
close to Jesus all their lives. I wonder if this letter ever
reached him. Perhaps the Reds got it instead. Then we
asked God to enlighten our minds to show us what we
should do in order to be prepared for the worst.

My mother's report continues: *Stan is feeling*
responsible for all the hospital staff. He was able to find
places of escape from the hospital. As I was walking in
the garden with him, we wondered where we as a family
could hide. He mentioned the dry well, but it looks so
deep and dark that I shuddered. I should not like to be
shut up in it with three small children. Our best plan
was to create a secret place in the house. We bricked up a
doorway which led into two old storerooms in the corner
of the courtyard. The only way of reaching them would
then be by scrambling onto the kitchen roof, over a small
sloping roof, and across the great main roof which was
large and sloped quite sharply, so much so that a
terrorist might well hesitate to walk on it. At the other
end a ladder would be standing, down which we could
climb to the walled in courtyard, the only access to our
secret. We furnished these two rooms with a bed, some
mattresses, boxes for storing bedding and food, a stove
and a chimney, a chair and stools, wash basin, pails, a
candle and matches, and paper and pencils for the
children. We also put in a store of coal, kindling and
paper and a water barrel while a local bricklayer blocked
off the entrance from the house.

We are a bit anxious about this as he is a talkative old
man. It is impossible to do anything secretly in this

country. The bricklayer thinks that we want to put our treasures there and so we do, for our children are our treasures. Mary is perfectly sweet about it all. She is the only child who can understand. Having heard all about Peter Pan and the Pirates, it seems to her as if she were living in an exciting book. She skips along over the roof, climbs boldly down the ladder, and helps me put away all sorts of useful things. We practiced climbing over the roof with John, aged 2½, and Elizabeth as a baby in our arms.

The trouble was that to get to the secret rooms we had to climb over a roof that was visible from the city gates, so there was the danger of being seen by the terrorists or townsfolk friendly toward them. The city was closely shut up for two weeks, and there must have been real fear of mayhem. My father quietly prepared for the worst. I dimly remember the secret room and the idea of keeping it secret but was totally unaware of the fact that I could have been orphaned or killed at any time.

A remarkable coincidence occurred which we only discovered much later at a family reunion. My mother put in her diary that they had received a telegram from their friend Miss Deck, who wrote *We go Kaifeng. Yuincheng evacuated.* This turned out to be Phyllis Deck, my wife Luci's aunt. She died while trying to escape the terrorists. Amazingly, our city was never attacked though enemy forces came within a mile of the gates. We were saved.

Whether it was because of continuing danger or other factors, the family finally left Linfen, where Dad had practiced medicine for twenty-one years. Certainly part of the reason was to keep our large family together in that very unstable era. We moved to Chefoo, the seaside town where my brothers had already been going to boarding school. It was a mission school, founded in 1881 and run on British "Public School" (which means *private boarding school*) lines, with cricket in the summer, soccer, rowing, and a mission-focused Christian faith. Academically, it was considered the best British school east of Suez. Thornton Wilder and Henry Luce, founder of *Life* magazine, had both attended it. The graduating exams were created and tested at Oxford. With Dad working at the city hospital, we were together at last as a family.

During a brief vacation Mom and Dad took down the coast, we were taken care of by Gladys Aylward, a remarkable and courageous missionary who was a close family friend and had stayed with us in Linfen. She became a Chinese citizen to identify with the people, and rescued over a hundred orphan children from the Japanese advance by leading them over two mountain ranges and the Yellow River.

The next year, the Japanese army moved into town and life became more uncertain. But there was very little resistance in Chefoo, though there were nights with gunfire from pockets of local Chinese militia. As neutral British citizens, we were not affected much.

I was four when Mom and Dad were called to Tientsin to help after devastating flooding of the Yellow River left thousands of Chinese drowned or without homes. They took Elizabeth and me with them, and I well recall waiting at a railway station, guarding several pieces of luggage, with Elizabeth at one end and me at the other, while Mom and Dad tried to settle passport problems. I held my breath in apprehension and put up a simple child's prayer—perhaps my first remembered prayer.

Nothing was stolen while they were gone. We loaded the luggage into the train and were off. Arriving well after midnight, I was very pleased that I was wide awake and, in a sense, treated like an adult. Tientsin was in desperate need, with thousands of refugees and nowhere to provide them shelter from the bitter winter. We came upon a vast field of refugee huts, and Dad climbed down into them to inspect the miserable conditions. I went into one after him, wearing a mask. The smell was terrible. No heat, no sanitation, and imminent danger of typhus.

LOST IN SHANGHAI AT AGE FIVE

That summer we went for a holiday to Shanghai. There was great excitement, as we were going to the big city for the first time. One day as Dad was taking all of us kids to the park to play, he pointed out that my shoelace was undone. I knelt down to tie it, and when I looked up after struggling for a few minutes, everyone had disappeared. Probably Dad had assumed I'd fix the lace when we got to the park, and had gone on with the other kids. There I was in the middle of bustling Shanghai, completely lost. Little did I realize the danger, as I could easily have been kidnapped and held for ransom.

Fortunately, an apparently wealthy and, to me, stylish Chinese lady took my hand and paid a rickshaw coolie to take me to the police station. I was too scared to thank her, and sat, small and lonely, in the middle of the wide rickshaw seat, wondering where I was being sent. The rickshaw was old and rickety. The seat smelled of tobacco and grease. I watched the back of the runner's neck where little beads of sweat were appearing as he hurried along. I felt completely helpless. He could have kidnapped me or dumped me anywhere. I gripped the arms of the rickshaw and prayed. The police station seemed a long way off, but we eventually got there. He took my arm and hurried me through the swinging doors with a sigh of relief. It was as if he had been protecting me from some invisible terror out on the streets. Clearly he felt responsible for me and handed me over to a British policeman.

I was relieved to hear English spoken and simply sobbed, "I want my mother." I was told to sit on a little stool in the main reception room. A policeman towered over me on a high stool asking questions and making notes in his pad. The smell of the cigar he was smoking coming down to me from on high. Being lost was a completely new experience. During what seemed an eternity of waiting, I wrestled with the idea. It was partly fear but also an adventure into the unknown. I couldn't put the two emotions together and began to cry.

Then, wonder of wonders, my mother came advancing toward me from across the room. When I saw her face, I realized I was found. Oh the magic of that moment. It was her face, her radiant face that transformed me. I will never, ever forget it. It seemed better to have been lost and then found than not to have been lost at all. After that first flush of joy, I thought more about the experience and have come to believe there was something unique about being lost. It is more a matter of relationship than of location. Life was wonderful and new again. In fact, I felt I was living a strangely new life. I had survived the abyss and was all the more certain of my mother's love. If I could be rescued from the streets of Shanghai, then I could be rescued from anywhere. This gave me a new sense of self-confidence. I wonder what my parents said to each other that evening!

While in Shanghai, we went to see the movie *Snow White and the Seven Dwarfs*, which gave me nightmares for some time afterward because of the images of the wicked queen. Then I remember the sensation of riding an escalator at a fancy, downtown shop and marveling at the upward movement. It was silent and so magical. Perhaps it would take me up to heaven.

Furlough to England

That fall I had just turned five. Mom and Dad took Elizabeth and me on their furlough to England. It must have been hard for my other siblings to be left in boarding school while we enjoyed the luxury of a long boat trip and the adventure of being with grandparents. I discovered years later that my sister Mary, aged seven at the time, was particularly hurt by being left in boarding school. Why didn't Mom and Dad bring her along with us? It would seem obvious in today's world, but there must have been other factors beyond my knowledge.

On the ship, there was a fancy dress party for which Elizabeth dressed up as a primrose while I was a bluebell. There were also rich foods that I was not used to, seasickness in the Mediterranean, and visits to Egypt and Palestine which I cannot remember.

At Dad's mother's home in Nottingham, we were happy to settle into the big rambling house. Our bedroom was on the third floor, with the bathroom and Grandma's bedroom one floor below. On the wall outside the bathroom was an Old Testament scene that terrified me: a man frantically knocking at the gates of a city he had fled to. In the distance, a crowd of wild figures wielding weapons was chasing him, but it looked as if he might be able to escape just in time. The picture scared the living daylights out of me, and whenever I went down to the bathroom, I would run past it with dread. Was I the man trying to escape to safety? Would the gates be opened in time?

While Mom and Dad went off for a short holiday with my grandmother in Wales, Elizabeth and I were left in a children's home in South London. We were miserable and missed our parents terribly. What is remarkable is that the home was run by two wonderful, loving ladies, Gwen Packer and Eileen Drake, who had felt called to care for missionary children that often were left with them at as early an age as two while their parents went overseas for long periods. We were the lucky one who only had two weeks' separation, while others ended up feeling closer to *Packie* and *Drakins* than to their own parents. After World War II, we were to get to know Packie and Drakins in a special way.

In London, I got to see the coronation of King George VI, as Dad put me on his shoulders to see the royal coach go by. Always the explorer willing to think outside the box, he somehow was able to get behind Buckingham Palace into the area where the coaches and horses were kept on the day before the coronation and take pictures of the coach being polished and spruced up. How proudly he showed us the photographs. Daddy's Leica was his constant joy, and our family has many negatives of pictures he took in China and elsewhere.

Grandpa Robert Wilder and Grandma Helene Olsson Wilder each had a claim to fame. My mother's parents had retired to Norway, where they lived in a big, rambling whitewashed house in a village near Lake Mjosa, north of Oslo. Grandpa Robert Wilder was American, a cousin to Almanzo Wilder whose wife, Laura Ingalls Wilder, wrote *Little House on the Prairie*. As a student at Princeton University, he had been co-founder of the Student Volunteer Movement, whose efforts led more than twenty thousand young people to serve overseas. I remember Grandpa as gentle and loving. He died later that year, 1937. Grandma Helene Olsson was motherly—like a big-bosomed thrush, as Dylan Thomas would put it—and welcomed us with open arms.

The magic of the family warmth and the Norwegian countryside is with me still when I recall our stay in a small garden guesthouse with a bright red door. My mother's aunt, Tanta Aagot, never married and became a famous painter. I still have her oil painting of the red door, surrounded by lush greenery. Grandma Helene's brother Willhelm was commander-in-chief of the Norwegian army during the 1905 war in which the country won independence from Sweden. How proud we were that we were related to him.

One evening, I was allowed to stay up late even though I was only five and go out with the farm workers to collect the hay. Just as it was getting to be dusk, I rode into town on the top of a huge cart piled fifteen feet high with hay and drawn by two magnificent horses. My joy was doubled as not only was I king of the road but in addition, my sister had been too young to be out on this adventure. Oh, the joy of feeling one up on a sibling!

The Halcyon Days of Chefoo

We returned to Chefoo by Christmas, and it was glorious being a whole family again with big brothers and sister to look up to and try and keep up with. Those nearly three years, from Christmas 1937 until the autumn of 1940, were the happiest time of my childhood. Dad had various jobs as school doctor, at a sanitarium, or elsewhere, and was able to help out in emergencies around the country. He wrote after helping at Kaifeng that he was "rioted out of the town."

Meanwhile, my mother made a remarkable and wonderful home for us six, with Dad joining in as often as possible. In the winters, we played our favorite gramophone records, and she encouraged us to dance around the table to ballet music. Many locals were invited home and warmly welcomed as friends and equals. It was a very open-house affair, and we could invite our friends from school—poor, jealous boarders, alas—to come home with us for an overnight stay. At the Chinese New Year we could stay up late and watch a huge paper dragon weaving in and out among the crowd, and then the setting off hundreds of firecrackers.

Mom took us for walks onto the city wall, allowing us to climb "forbidden" lion statues. Mary, a year older than me, used to regularly climb a dangerously high tree in the garden. My brother Rupert, three years older than me, was allowed to catch scorpions in a glass tumbler and bring them into the house. Mom used to read us *The Jungle Book, Black Beauty,* and other classics. Right from those early days, she gave each of us one day of the week for our own when we could choose our favorite dessert. We often played *sardines in the dark*—or *black beast,* as it was sometimes called—which helped us lose our fear of the dark, and Mom and Dad would play right along with us. What else could they do with all the lights out? We'd end up in a giggling mass of hugging bodies. Each week we would have a "family night" in which each of us was encouraged to perform in front of the family, and Mom and Dad helped with costumes and makeup.

But even in the midst of joy, war loomed. One scary night, the Communists attacked the city. I recall the gunfire and flashing lights reflecting off the bedroom ceiling. It started after midnight with a couple of distant explosions. Then there were bursts of gunfire getting closer. Dad woke those of us kids who were still sleeping, and told us to get under our beds and away from the windows. It was a moment more of excitement than fear, and eventually I fell asleep, still under my bed, without even a pillow.

After a brief spell of being boarders at the mission school when Mom and Dad were off on a rescue trip, we rented a much bigger house just outside the mission compound. It was opposite some special trees that we called the Seven Tree Pass. The good climbers could get from one end to the other without touching the ground, despite a really scary part in the middle. Though I longed to be up there, I never qualified.

About that time, we adopted a couple of cute puppies, with each of us trying to be the first down to wake them in the mornings and sniff their rich puppy smell. Rupert developed a passion for collecting butterflies, and Mom and Dad hired a local carpenter to make him a beautiful glass-topped box for his collection, all displayed with wings spread out. I can still smell that camphor wood; it uniquely brings me back to China. I watched him with fascination and even caught a few butterflies myself. Mom and Dad introduced us to gardening, and our cabbages and carrots attracted lots of white butterflies. All of us were encouraged to have our own part of the garden where we could grow our own vegetables and flowers. I was just a beginner but could see how well my elder brothers and sister did and tried to catch up.

Our mother was enterprising and resourceful. While Dad was away on one of his medical trips, she introduced the family to Scouting. This was a brand-new idea for Chefoo families, and she pioneered it by making our family of six into a regular scout troop, calling us together with the call *Pack, Pack, Pack*. First, she wrote off to England for information on how to form a troop and lists of badges we could work for. She taught us semaphore which we used to signal each other from rocky knobs on our hilly walks up to the Ning Hi Gate and to Adam's Knob, the highest hill behind the town (which we called a mountain because it was a thousand feet above sea level). We had stalking games which she encouraged, and soon our friends wanted to join the troop. Mom got permission from the boarding school and started an official scout troop. Thus were sown the seeds of the Scout and Girl Guide troops which were such a success in the Weihsien prison camp. We were very proud that our mother had the imagination and enterprise to start the whole idea. Our father taught us first aid and bandaging, so that badge was easy to earn. For each of us, Mom went through the list of all the badges available and what we should work on first. Mary must have started being a Girl Guide by 1940, as Mom was sewing many badges onto her camelhair blanket by then. Our parents inspired us to dare and to be different, but they did it in an enthusiastic yet unobtrusive way.

On Sundays, we walked as a family all the way along the beachfront to the community church on Temple Hill, but we would leave much earlier than needed so that there would be time to go rock scrambling along the beach on the way. We kids would walk in front with Mom and Dad behind so that Dad's voice would carry as he told us tales of Greek legends and his travels. After church, over Sunday lunch, we would discuss the sermon. I remember insisting at lunch once that the preacher for the day had been wearing glasses, while my siblings all insisted that he hadn't. I was so adamant that I took on a bet and would not budge. A couple weeks later as we walked along the beach, we saw the preacher coming our way wearing his glasses! My sense of triumph stayed with me for quite a long time, and you can be sure I collected the money I had won!

To encourage us kids to have fun and meet people in the wider community outside the mission station, Mom and Dad paid the expensive subscription to join the Lido beach club where we could buy soft drinks, lounge around, and paddle on the bay in a canoe a boatman would take down to the beach. I was too young to really appreciate this, but the older boys lived it up to the hilt. One scary afternoon, an offshore breeze that turned into a powerful wind made Eric and Rupert struggle to keep from being blown clear across the bay to the Bluff five miles away.

Our friends at the boarding school were jealous of the "Hoyte Tribe" because of our enterprising adventures such as visiting a British warship anchored in the bay and camping out on the Lighthouse Islands.

The cruiser HMS *Dorsetshire* looked resplendent in the morning light that day when Mom and Dad spontaneously threw out the suggestion that we should visit it. We had no permission, and there was no direct communication between people in town and the captain. But the eight of us set out in a rowboat toward the magnificent ship half a mile away. I vividly remember my mother's wonderful mix of spontaneity and modesty. She was in a swimsuit when we set off but changed into blouse and skirt on the way, *to be more properly attired for the occasion*, and we all laughed. There was magic in that family laughter and the expectancy that this was going to be a real adventure.

When we drew near the enormous side of the cruiser, which seemed as high as a five-story building, we called up asking if we could visit. After a few minutes' hesitation, a long sloping ladder of steps was lowered, and the smiling face of the chief petty officer, in impeccably smart white uniform, greeted us as we clambered up onto the ship in our bare feet. We were treated like royalty, piped aboard, and shown all around the ship—the engine room, the bridge, and finally the captain's cabin. One sailor was assigned to scrub our soles clean of tar that had crept up between the slats of the deck before we entered the captain's quarters. He talked with Mom and Dad about adult things, life at Chefoo, and what the Japanese were doing in China.

I was more interested in what stood on the sideboard, a perfect model of the original HMS *Dorsetshire*, one of the ships Sir

Francis Drake had commanded in defeating the Spanish Armada in 1588. It was made of pure silver, with silver sails billowing. How could I ever forget it! As a bonus, we were towed back to shore by the ship's motor launch, at twenty knots. The sheer luxury of not having to row on top of the royal treatment onboard ship was indescribable. Such is grace—undeserved, unmerited, and given freely. We discussed the event that evening over supper and concluded that the sailors, from captain to able seamen, were all delighted to welcome a British family, especially one with children, so far from their own homes back in England and after months at sea. It became the talk of the school: *The Hoytes had done it again!*

THE ULTIMATE HOLIDAY

Dad persuaded the school administrator to lend us a four-oar rowboat and to have the weekly lighthouse supply launch tow us out to the mysterious Lighthouse Islands seven miles off the coast. None of us younger kids had ever been there. All they had been were tiny silhouettes on the horizon to the east. Dad had taken the three older boys there the summer before, but now it was our turn as a complete family to camp on the beach of one of the islands for a whole two weeks. How did our parents manage to pack all the equipment into an open rowboat?

That was the last summer together before Mom and Dad left us at the boarding school, so it was especially memorable. Mom did the cooking over charcoal on two earthenware braziers. We survived two storms during the fortnight, and I remember Dad and the older boys swimming out to the anchored boat to bring it back to shore when a heavy swell threatened. There were also blissful days of bright sunshine, swimming, and exploring the caves around the headland. We discovered an elephant rock on the other side of the island that the sea had carved a tunnel through, and navigated the boat through it to explore the rocky coast beyond. Dad had built a two-foot wooden box with a glass bottom so we could watch brilliantly colored fish underwater from the boat. Mom introduced us to watercolors there. I still have a beautiful watercolor of a breathtaking sunset that she painted as I sat beside her watching, helping me remember her as a spontaneous artist.

Our two weeks were over all too soon, and we were towed back to Chefoo with memories to last a lifetime. Back at school, my classmates asked me about the camp out, and I remember feeling totally inadequate to describe the closeness of the family and the excitement of our adventure together. I knew then that we were a special family and was proud of my parents. I was seven, about to turn eight.

On the island, Dad told us stories of his early adventures at Linfen. *Late one night he was called to the hospital on an emergency. A madman, seemingly possessed by a demon, was being held down by four strong men in the reception hall. Dad went to the pharmacy to get an injection needle and medicine to put him to sleep. By the time he came back, the man had gotten loose and, with superhuman strength, had broken off the top of the large potbellied stove in the center of the room. He was kneeling and about to put his face right into the red hot embers when Dad gently pulled him away. The man fought with him fiercely. Though Dad was no match for such a man, he strongly believed that the power of God was with him, and he was able to hold the man down. Somehow Dad was able to subdue and sedate him.* Such was the life of a medical missionary, and we children were proud that we were part of his courageous family. We began to see his life as one of considerable danger.

My chief hobby was collecting keys, of all shapes and sizes. They would hang from a ring on my waist, and whenever I found a locked door or a discarded padlock I would set to work to see if I had a key that would fit it. Wherever I went there would be a jingling sound. My siblings found this amusing, and my nickname became "John Klink." I still sign my family emails that way.

Only they know why! This tendency of wanting to know "what is behind that door" became a very strong instinct which has been both a blessing and a curse. It has gotten me into trouble several times but also has led to positive risk-taking and growth in wisdom.

THE COMING DARKNESS

Maybe you have to know the darkness before you appreciate the light.
—Madeleine L'Engle

In September of 1940, when I was just eight years old and still carrying my many keys around, Mom and Dad were asked to set out from Chefoo to Lanchow, over thirteen hundred miles away in the northwestern province of Kansu, to aid with a mission hospital crisis. They reluctantly accepted the challenge. For them, the journey would cover more like fifteen hundred miles, crossing over three flooded parts of the Yellow River as well as the no-man's-land between the Japanese and Chinese armies. Much of this was by foot, cart, wheelbarrow, and boat, putting them in danger from bandits, guerrillas, drug smugglers, snipers, and military red tape. After three months, they reached their destination, and later published a booklet describing their adventures, with sketches my mother made along the way. Perhaps that is what inspired me to always carry a little sketchbook when on vacation and to maintain a sketching journal.

With six children at the school, our parents had asked the mission leaders if they could remain at Chefoo, but Dad was badly needed to be superintendent of the hospital at Lanchow. Looking back, how we wished that he had said "no" and insisted on either staying at Chefoo or, if that did not work out for the mission, taking us all back to England for our education. Hindsight is easy, but at the time, missionaries seldom questioned the decisions of their mission board. Also, little did we know of the coming attack on Pearl Harbor, and there were certainly expectations that we would be together for another Chefoo holiday in the foreseeable future. Our mother hated to show us children how much she felt the parting. She did not want to add to our distress, so spoke brightly of the holidays we would have together in the future. Yet as she left Elizabeth, her youngest, she completely broke down in the headmistress's room after saying goodbye. It took great courage to compose herself and face the future.

So it was that we were orphaned for five years, for instead of seeing Mom and Dad the next summer as anticipated, we faced a Japanese internment camp. My brother Rupert later wrote about his sadness when told that we would be taking up boarding again at school. The devotion that our parents had to their missionary calling had always seemed to him so totally genuine and of over-riding importance that he thought he could honestly say he never really resented it. In this, he considered himself most fortunate, knowing that many children of missionaries have continued through life with much resentment. That was Rupert's response.

Family portrait just before Mom and Dad left for Lanchow. How sad we looked! We never saw Mom again.

However, each of us six responded differently, and we have all had to struggle over the separation—a full five years from our father and forever from our mother, or at least for this lifetime.

I was still at the prep school and felt particularly lonely and sad that first Christmas after Mom and Dad left. The teachers did their best to comfort Elizabeth and me, but we needed the family comfort that no boarding school could supply. Our siblings were separated from us in the upper grades, and the boys' and girls' schools were in different buildings. One huge encouragement for me was that Miss Stark, who taught art and literature, praised my drawing abilities and encouraged me to draw and color a Christmas card for my parents. Her enthusiasm was infectious. I suddenly experienced a new sense of self-worth in spite of the loss of Mom and Dad and our close-knit family unit. This made a huge difference to me at this crucial time in my life.

Most of my experiences in the prep school were with other boys and girls my age, and I do not recall spending time with my older brothers and sister. This was one of the problems of boarding school life. Siblings tended to be separated by grade and so lose family cohesion. We used to explore the hills behind Chefoo, and at one point, three of us found a low, narrow tunnel in the foothills. Smaller friends managed to get through, but I became stuck at a very narrow point and panicked. The experience of lying there in complete darkness unable to move forward or backward was terrifying. Praying calmed me down, and inch by inch I worked my way backward and out again with just a few scratches. The experience fits so well into my theme of light and its corollary darkness. The dark, coupled with total immobility, became synonymous, a kind of paralysis. That fit my mental state.

There were times when we *prepites* were quite rebellious, and once, a group of us sat in the school's central courtyard refusing to move or obey any of our teachers' requests. I do not recall what the outward reason for the revolt was, and on the whole, the teachers were loving and patient with us. But they were not our parents, and so for all this time, we had a deep ache inside. Now I understand it as a sign of the shades of darkness and separation we all were experiencing.

THE STORM STRIKES

> *Forget your perfect offering.*
> *There is a crack in everything*
> *That's how the light gets in.*
>
> —Leonard Cohen

It was December of 1941, and I was walking along the beach with some friends. Out to sea a huge storm was gathering with dark and sinister clouds. A stiff salt wind was springing up, and I suddenly felt chilled. The storm was moving quickly in our direction, and we began to look for cover. An older boy ran up to us shouting:

> *Have you heard? The Japs have attacked the American*
> *fleet at Pearl Harbor, and we are at war with Japan.*

How does a nine-year-old boy react to such news? I immediately connected it with the storm at sea and felt a simultaneous sensation of dread and excitement. A huge storm was coming, and we would be caught up in it. I felt dread at what the Japanese might do to us and excitement at the possibility of adventure in this new, unpredictable world. Danger thrummed through my being as my friends and I scurried for cover.

A few days later, we had another surprise. Along the main road into town came several hundred Japanese cavalry in double file. At first, we just heard the clip-clop of hooves, and then turned wide-eyed to the improbable scene.

It was vivid: The harnesses jingled, horses whinnied, the smell of horse manure wafted on the air. The leader shouted strange commands in Japanese, and each rider wore a long curved sword.

It seemed like a war movie projecting me back into World War I. But it was real. I now realized that indeed, we were enemy aliens. The United States and Britain both had declared war on Japan, and life under Japanese control would be quite different from now on. Our headmaster Mr. Bruce, was taken into custody for a month, and our ability to travel out of the mission compound was restricted. We had to wear armbands wherever we went. The teachers began to prepare us for the tough time ahead. At that moment, I wished Mom and Dad were not so far away but right here with us at Chefoo. I was an orphan placed twice into jeopardy. It was dark. The storm had hit.

Temple Hill Internment

Eventually, the Japanese military took over the whole school compound, and the two hundred students and teachers were forced to move to Temple Hill on the other side of town, into three houses built to each house a family of six. We managed to squeeze into them and every square inch was precious. After we had been marched out of our old school buildings and had a chance to look around, it was discovered that all the light bulbs had been stolen from our new confinement. My oldest brother, Robin, had the presence of mind to somehow sneak back into the school and fill an old suitcase with as many light bulbs as he could find. When the Japanese guard challenged him as he left the compound, he just replied with a nonchalant *beerdee dungshee,* meaning that he had *some things.* Amazingly, he was not searched, and we enjoyed the benefits of his courage for many months to come. How proud I was of my big brother! During those sardine months on Temple Hill, food became very scarce not only in our camp but also in town. The Japanese commandant was a Christian and could give us more food than was available to the townsfolk, including German and Italian missionaries who, of course, were not imprisoned.

This raised an interesting question: How did we as proudly
British missionaries and "mishkids" relate to missionaries from
enemy countries? I am thankful to say that generally, we treated
each other with goodwill and respect. However, I do recall that
before Mom and Dad left, a German missionary family living
next door repeatedly sang nationalistic German songs. We were
duly distressed but kept this to ourselves like good Christians.
Our thoughts were not so holy!

Since the walls around our makeshift camp were only six feet
high, it would have been easy to escape. But as conditions were
worse outside than inside, we naturally didn't. In fact, the reverse
took place. Chinese thieves would climb in and take what they
could. This led to my first attempt at writing a brief memoir, complete with sketches of the camp compound and a thief climbing
down from a veranda:

THIEVES

*There are a number of Chinese people who live in
some houses just behind our camp, and they can see very
well onto our verandahs. They watched where we kept
things, and they knew that on the front and side
verandahs, there were rows of boxes. They decided that
they would come and steal a lot of things. June 15. In the
early morning of Foundation Day the big boys were
sleeping in the garden when a thief crept up to our
verandah. Costerus heard him and called out, first in
English and then in Chinese. Then he sent Theo Bazire to
tell Mr. Bazire that there was a thief. Costerus himself
went to the kitchen to get a mop. The thief heard some
noises, so he thought he would go down the stairs. But
luckily Mr. Bazire was at the bottom, so he went back
onto the verandah and climbed down a pillar and ran.
The boys saw him and gave chase. The man tripped up
and was taken to the boys' room as a captive. They tied*

him up and took him to the laundry room. They gave him
a mattress and drink. Mr. Bazire sat outside, guarding
him in a deck chair, and at 5:30 AM, he went to light the
kitchen fire. Before he went, he loosened the man's hands
"to make him feel more comfortable." Then he left a boy to
keep guard on the thief. The thief slipped his hands out of
the loops where his wrists were tied and moved a tub to
get out of the window. When he was out, he climbed over
a wall, so he escaped after all. All the grownups were very
relieved for they thought he would be hurt by the
Japanese if we handed him over.

Such is the situation when a compassionate missionary cap-
tures a thief under an authoritarian dictatorship! I cannot remember if the Japanese commandant was a Christian at this
stage or not.

Gate to Freedom: The Japanese Prison Camp at Weihsien.

WEIHSIEN INTERNMENT CAMP

The news came through that we were to be moved to a much bigger prison camp at Weihsien, a hundred fifty miles inland. The journey there involved two stages, first to Tsingtao by steamer and then by rail. The Japanese officials did not provide any food for the two-day journey but allowed us to order bread. This was to be the mainstay of the voyage, since we would be completely out of other food. The baker who delivered bread to the camp agreed to deliver it directly to the Japanese ship. However, our hearts sank as the boat left the dock before the baker arrived. By God's grace, the boat had to drop anchor out in the bay for a few minutes, letting the baker secure a rowboat and deliver the bread just in time!

There were three hundred of us crowded into the hundred-fifty-foot steamer. With no cabins and only bare decks, the school staff and children were allotted the hold for sleeping quarters. We lay head to tail like sardines, or shoulder to shoulder, on the flat boarding, with not an inch to spare. No toilet facilities were provided. By the second day, the smell became horrendous. The hatches were battened down at night, and no one was allowed on deck.

There wasn't much sleeping, and on the second night, I managed to slip out through a carelessly unlocked hatch to the blissful coolness of the deck. It must have been about midnight. I was restless and hungry but elated at having escaped the "dungeon." Moving forward to the prow of the ship, all alone, I sat with my feet dangling over the edge, my legs on either side of the steel cable that stretched up from the bow to the top of the foremast. With a full moon above and a moonlit path rippling to the deep blue horizon, I seemed to be looking out into infinity. Gone was the hunger. Gone was the fear, even though we were going through mine-infested waters. Gone was the sense of being deserted by my parents. I felt surrounded by a sense of complete love and peace. The writer C.S. Lewis has described moments in his life of inexplicable wonder, of longing, of beauty and awe.

This was my moment. The experience was a mountain peak in my life's journey. I was loved, and the rippled moonlight seemed a pathway to peace.

Dawn of the second day brought us to Tsingtao, and we spent a long, hot, waterless day on the train to Weihsien. Many lost their luggage on the way, and boxes and suitcases were broken open and rifled. Finally, tired and disheveled, we piled onto flatbed trucks and were brought the final two miles to the camp at what had been a Presbyterian mission compound. Before we arrived, though, the school, seminary, church, and hospital had been completely trashed, wrecked by several garrisons of Chinese and Japanese soldiers.

Fortunately for us, an earlier band of prisoners from Beijing and Tientsin had worked on improving matters, cleaning out the toilets (which were inches thick in human waste), and establishing two working kitchens. Our new home was about two hundred by a hundred fifty yards, and housed up to two thousand prisoners at its maximum. There were rows and rows of tiny rooms which had been designated for Chinese students, each with a narrow door and window at the front and a small window at the rear, but now were crammed with prisoner families. With no running water or heat, the new inmates had to become very adaptable.

Six months earlier, the first batch had been brought in, followed by group after group of enemy nationals, as the Japanese called us, from many parts of northern China. Before our three hundred arrived, there were about sixteen hundred prisoners. It was a crowd of many nationalities, the very last arrivals being Italians brought in after their country's capitulation. Together, they all formed a mixed bag of personalities, rich and poor, missionary and secular, young and old, generous and miserly, healthy and sick. Mr. Watham, for example, was a millionaire, the president of a huge coal mining operation, while Barbey was a drug addict picked up off the streets of Beijing. We all had to learn to live within the same primitive conditions.

We climbed off the trucks at the main gate and staggered up Main Street, carrying or lugging our boxes and suitcases. The dusty, unpaved road was later called *Montgomery's Ride*, with the unlikely British hope that some day, General Montgomery of El Alamein would ride into camp to set us free. The internees already there were crowding the walls, the gates, and the alleys to welcome us. Pity, interest, curiosity, and perhaps a little disgust at the thought of more mouths to feed were all evident on their faces. Their clothes looked rumpled and torn, covered with dust and dirt, but there were women and children as well as men.

We kids were excited at the prospect of more space to run around in after being cramped for so long in the three houses in Chefoo. The housing committee found space for us in the education building. We had to make do with what bedding we had, as our mattresses did not arrive for another two weeks. We unpacked and settled down on the floor. Apprehension and excitement kept me awake for some time. Next morning, we explored our new environment. High walls surrounded the camp, with guard towers at each strategic corner, and high voltage wires, mounted on insulators, warning us against any attempt to escape. There also were searchlights and guard dogs, and we wisely respected the security that surrounded us.

Slowly we began to understand how things were run. The Japanese had told the first prisoners that they would be left to themselves and would have to organize the camp without Japanese supervision. Our guards would provide the basics for survival: food, heat in the winter (mostly coal dust), electricity, and waste removal. Committees were elected so that the camp became a democracy within the larger totalitarian governance. There was a housing committee to find a home for every new prisoner, an employment committee to give everyone a job, and a discipline committee to keep order and prevent the Japanese guards getting involved.

My first experience with the discipline committee came when my friend Theo and I were reported to the committee for throwing stones at the insulators on top of the outside walls. It was a thoughtless thing to do, for the insulators were the foundational building blocks of the security system. If the Japanese guards had caught us, we might have been severely punished. Luckily, our punishment was relatively benign, writing out several hundred times *I must not throw stones at the wall-top insulators.* As we were desperately short of paper, I cannot recall how we found the means to do this, but I am grateful that we were not punished more severely.

Langdon Gilkey, later the author of *Shantung Compound,* the most definitive book on our camp, was a member of the housing committee. He wrote about the problem of cramming two thousand people into our limited space. The spacious homes of the directors and staff of the original Presbyterian school had been taken over by our captors, while we were crammed into the tight little rooms designed for students. Every time our captors summoned the housing committee and blithely announced that another batch of prisoners was coming to the camp, it was up to the committee and not the guards to find space for them. Guards can command and threaten. Fellow internees can only ask, cajole and persuade.

JOBS AND WATER

Everyone had a job—even the slackers, and there always were some, who tried their best to get away with as little work as possible. We kids watched the adults laboring away in the kitchens and janitorial services, making shelving and stovepipes, and providing many other services, and wondered how we could contribute. Eventually, we were given our own jobs. Mine, as an eleven-year-old, was to work the manual water pump for an hour at a time. All the water for the camp was pumped up by hand from two deep wells into two thirty-foot water towers. Fortunately we never ran out of water. Our pump was a long-levered, double-handled type, made of cast iron and creaking loudly as we operators moved the handles up and down. For a whole hour we would work at it, with short breaks or taking it in turns. The book lovers would be able to place a book beside the mechanism and read it while pumping. I tried to read *The Scarlet Pimpernel* this way. It worked for a while but my eyes would get tired refocusing all the time.

We climbed up the metal ladder fastened to the side of the water tower and gaze longingly at the cool liquid glory up there, in the sweltering heat of summer. Oh for a dip! This was, of course, strictly forbidden. I cannot remember the punishment but it must have been severe as not once did our little gang of eleven-and-twelve-year-olds go in. The wells were contaminated with giardia, so all drinking water had to be boiled. On long, hot summer days we would drink and drink and drink, mainly from old wine bottles, though the water was always lukewarm. All the refrigerators that were in the compound had been taken by the Japanese.

My ten-year-old sister, Elizabeth, had the job of hanging out laundry to dry. During the summer this was fine, but in the bitter cold winters, her fingers turned black and blue. It was particularly painful gathering in the sheets that turned into solid expanses of ice on the clotheslines. Cleanliness was a constant challenge, as soap was desperately short in supply. We were supposed to receive one small bar per person per month, but delivery was unreliable, the quality of soap was bad, and it had to cover all laundry, personal toilet, and cleaning facilities. Eventually whites took on a permanent grayness. After a few months, linens, socks, and other clothing became worn and torn, making repairing them a major project for the women and girls. I was quite expert at darning my own socks, a practice I had learned from my mother. Everything was recycled. Everything was hand-me-down. We were growing out of the clothes we had at the beginning of the war. I became well acquainted with my brothers' things.

Leather was scarce and shoes precious. We went barefoot as much of the year as possible, definitely all summer and as much of the spring and fall as we could. The camp shoe repair shop was much appreciated when leather started to fall apart.

ENCOUNTERS WITH DEATH

Although our camp was very different from those run by the Japanese military in the south, Hong Kong, Singapore, and the Philippines, where prisoners were treated worse than animals, the presence of death and the vulnerability of life was always with us. My first encounter with a dead human was soon after we had arrived at Weihsien.

Theo and I were exploring the nooks and crannies of our new prison home when we saw the door ajar on a little, windowless hut tucked away on the far side of the hospital. Not knowing what to expect, we ventured in and found the body of a woman, clearly a beautiful, young nun, lying on a central, raised dais, dressed in her full habit with hands together in a position of prayer. Theo and I stood in silence, breathless and awestruck. I asked myself, *What is this state of being called death?* My parents had taught me that when we die, we go to be with Jesus. This nun then must be with Jesus but had left behind her silent, alabaster body. Her face, so young and beautiful, made it all the more difficult to understand how death could affect youth so quickly.

When children look on a human death, they instinctively know the terrible difference between this and that of a favorite pet. Some children would have wanted to get out of the morgue as soon as possible. I wanted to stay. I carefully touched the hem of the nun's habit as an act of reaching out to the mystery, to the unknown, though I did not know where it would lead. Here was a mystery, and I was on the shore of a vast unknown ocean. Little did I know that—twelve months in the future and thirteen hundred miles away—my own mother's body would lie like this, with my dad watching over her, his life torn apart in grief. Theo and I left in silence, not saying a word. We had ventured out of our depth.

My second encounter with death happened six months later. Twice a day, the Japanese guards took a roll call of all prisoners to ensure that there were no escapees. We were each allocated a number in Japanese. Mine was twenty-two, *ni-joo-ni*, and after we had formed into a long line, I would shout out my number when my turn came. The sequential callout of numbers is still firmly embedded in my brain, with the different pitches of boys', girls', and adult voices making a rhythmic tune.

A power line to the searchlight in a corner watchtower crossed diagonally across the parade ground. For some reason, its anchoring had slipped so that its sagging center was about seven feet from the ground. As we were assembling, a boy reached up, touched the uninsulated wire and exclaimed on getting an electric shock, *Wow! That's hot!* Inexplicably, his schoolmate, Brian, a friend of mine, grabbed the wire and was immediately electrocuted. As with all of us in the summer, he was barefoot and so had no insulation from the damp ground.

I was about twenty feet away and did not see what was happening but sensed the panic and fear radiating outward. Someone held back Brian's horrified mother from running forward and holding him. No one could touch Brian or detach his hand from the wire for fear of death, but at last, someone used an umbrella to release him from the power line. He was taken immediately to the hospital, but nothing could save him because of the time it had taken to free him—about thirty seconds which seemed like hours. Our close proximity to the tragedy, both physically and through friendship, had turned the experience into a communal death. I had been brought into the very act of a friend's dying. It was hard to talk about afterward, though our teachers did their best, and we were left with a wound that festered for months.

The third brush with death was when another friend, Ronny Masters, age eighteen, fell forty feet from a tree when a branch gave way. Several bones were broken, and we who were living on the attic floor of the hospital could hear his cries of agony all night long. No pain relief medicines were available, and he died the next morning. What hit us so hard about Ronny's passing is that he was one of our heroes—strong, virile, a superb specimen of physical beauty—and now he was gone. I still have a sketch of his profile in my sketchbook, a reminder to me that *sketching is remembering*.

The fourth death hit us hardest of all. Eric Liddell had won a gold medal for Britain in the 1924 Olympics by winning the 40 meter run although he had trained for another race, which he did not want to run on a Sunday as it was the Lord's day to be kept holy. He was extremely modest about his gold medal. Now he was a missionary in China and had already shown courage before ever entering Weihsien. The Japanese had left a poor Chinese man dying after trying to behead him in a deserted temple in no-man's-land during Sino-Japanese fighting. Eric got a Chinese friend to go with him, found a wheelbarrow, and crossed the dangerous fighting lines to bring the man back to a hospital and save his life. Afterward, Eric found that he was a brilliant artist and kept one of his paintings, a pink and white peony, over his bed in the camp. He was as close to being a saint as one could imagine. Overflowing with good humor and love of life, Eric devoted his time to us young people. He organized games, particularly field hockey, planned square dances, chess tournaments, and debates, and was tireless in living out the life of Christ for others.

My eldest brother Robin slept in the same dormitory as Eric. He pointed out the painting during one of my visits and introduced me to Eric. He was forty-two, with a spring in his step and a friendly smile. I was eleven and feeling quite insignificant. Eric spoke to me with such ease and informality that I suddenly felt joy. That was his nature, for he loved kids and would do anything he could to give us orphans, separated from our parents, a sense of self-worth in spite of the misery of the camp. If we were without Mom and Dad, he was without his wife and daughters, who were now in Canada, so he understood our longings. It became apparent that for him, the three and a half years of confinement were the very opposite of being wasted. There was no difference between the secular and the sacred. We called him Uncle Eric.

Quite suddenly, he developed extreme headaches, and died of a brain tumor within four days. Everyone loved him, particularly us kids, and the shock to the whole camp was extreme. I remember the gray, winter day of his burial. I was a member of the boys honor guard at the gravesite just outside the camp walls. The bleak treeless landscape fit the sadness of the occasion. The award-winning movie *Chariots of Fire* was made about his life. When I saw it, I compared that primitive burial with the grand memorial service in St. Paul's Cathedral for the other runner in the film. Of course, older folk were dying all the time as the war continued, conditions deteriorated, food became scarcer, and medicines less available, but those four deaths were close to the bone for me.

Sketching, Food, and Fuel

With a lot of time on my hands, I began to sketch, and found that there was quite an artists' colony in camp to encourage us beginners. Tommy Knott had been a professional cartoonist before the war. My brother Rupert was taking lessons from him. I benefited greatly as Tommy's clever techniques were passed on to me. I also began filling a small sketchbook with drawings of camp buildings, portraits of friends, and, for want of a more-interesting subject, innumerable drawings of my left hand. Seventy years later, I still have my little sketchbook, faded, manhandled, and torn but still intact.

Camp life revolved around food and fuel, food to keep us going and fuel to keep us warm. Both were the cause of much turmoil and anguish, and lack of them the cause of much suffering. The food in the camp was prepared, cooked, and distributed in two kitchens. We children went to Kitchen #1 which fed up to a thousand prisoners. The staple and generally unappetizing diet was a coarse, peasant grain called *kaoliang*. There was kaoliang soup, kaoliang porridge, kaoliang stew, and kaoliang curry, and not much else.

The meat we had was from horses or mules, and so tough it needed a lot of cooking. Because there was no refrigeration, meat had to be cooked as soon as possible, and, of course, there was never enough to go around, particularly for us growing boys. Since ten pounds of meat would have to feed a thousand internees, the cooks would make it into a thin but at least slightly meaty stew. Such things as milk, eggs, and sugar were considered luxuries and kept for expectant mothers or the very ill. Near the end of the war, food became harder and harder to get, strongly tempting the workers who handled it to steal. When you are putting the ten pounds of meat into the huge cooking pot for your thousand impersonal campers while your own, close family is starving, it would be easy to cut off a half pound slice and slip it into a pocket. This raised the whole question of personal morality in a situation where everything of value was scarce.

I would like to say that the Christians, and in particular the missionaries, were the most honest. However, it was not always so. I think of the famous couplet by Bertolt Brecht:

> *For even saintly folk will act like sinners*
> *Unless they have their customary dinners.*

For us kids, the daily eating procedure was boringly routine. Every morning, after Japanese roll call, we would race down to Kitchen #1 grasping our camp-fabricated tin mugs and plates. It made no sense that we hurried, as the fare was pretty much the same each morning, and the waiting line was just as long. This is what we were served:

■ Breakfast: kaoliang porridge, black tea, and bread.

■ Lunch: Curry or stew (kaoliang with any meat available), black tea, and bread.

■ Supper: Soup, black tea, bread, and cake if we were lucky.

The evening's soup nearly always turned out to be the leftover stew watered down to make it go further. The more enterprising cooks occasionally baked what we liked to call cake, made of local saltana raisins, flour, and peanut oil.

We were desperately short of green vegetables, and there was an attempt to grow a vegetable garden at the back of the camp. But space was so limited that it did not amount to much. To help our bones grow, so ran the theory, we children were required to eat a daily teaspoon of powdered egg shells to make up for the milk we were not getting. How we loathed the flat, dry, choking taste. We never found out where the shells came from as we did not see many eggs in our diet. Fruit was nonexistent. Norman Cliff, a close friend of my brother Robin, was invited to play chess with one of the Japanese officers. As they played, in the relatively luxurious Officers' Quarters, the officer handed him an apple, an inch and a half across. Norman devoured it, small though it was. It was the only fruit he had tasted during his years in the camp. He was also suffering from amoebic dysentery and backaches, attributed to the lack of hygiene and hard labor at the camp.

Six months before the end of the war, yeast became unobtainable, so the bakery was unable to produce bread. Considering how important it was to our limited diet, this meant we were near the starvation point. Day after day, the diary of my youngest sister, Elizabeth, read: *Still no bread*. Red Cross parcels came in the nick of time and helped us survive.

It amazes me still that, after years in confinement, we six siblings were relatively healthy when we were set free. However, we were thin, with my ribs quite visible. None of us had rickets or other effects of malnutrition, and our teeth were in excellent shape. Our U.K. dental checkup found not one cavity! Nevertheless, my lingering memory is of constantly feeling hungry after meals and trying to make up for it by drinking lots of water—lukewarm, of course, because it had to be boiled.

The longer the war lasted, the more selfish people became. The idea of all starting off on an even basis, with everyone sharing equally, or at least according to their need, faded along with the sense of community. The needs of the family unit or, ultimately, the individual person, took its place, so that everyone outside that personal circle inevitably suffered.

This was dramatically illustrated by an incident near the end of the war when food supplies were being drastically cut. A wonderful gift to the camp came in the form of two thousand Red Cross parcels from the U.S. made available through the Swiss consulate. They contained all the delicious foods we longed for: cheeses, raisins, chocolates, jam, coffee, milk powder, a can of peaches, and even chewing gum but clearly in limited quantities. The Japanese commandant announced the great day of distribution—*One parcel for every prisoner*—and as there were just eighteen hundred of us, the extra two hundred parcels would go to the two hundred Americans.

We Brits did not object until we learned that the Yanks had gone to the commandant claiming that according to western private property laws, all two thousand parcels belonged to them, receiving ten parcels each. Langdon Gilkey, an American on the housing committee, took a poll of the two hundred and found that most would not agree with the reasoning of sharing more equally. Even some missionaries rationalized that their needs were too great to think otherwise. Also, they argued, once they received their ten parcels each, they could show some charity in sharing with other prisoners.

The commandant, trying to understand this reasoning, sent off to the High Command in Tokyo for advice. Immediately, the Americans were persona non grata and scorned by the rest of us. They appeared to be selfish, gluttonous, and nationalistic. But they saw themselves as simply exercising their perfectly justifiable rights. Eventually, everyone got one parcel and the extra two hundred were sent to other prison camps. We Brits laughed at the Americans, but the hunger in the camp was so great that I now believe we would have behaved just as selfishly if in their shoes.

Winters in northern China can get well below freezing, and we faced the problem of keeping warm for what seemed like interminably long winters to us kids. Our fuel was coal dust, with a few chunks of solid coal occasionally thrown in. The Japanese provided the fuel while we had to design and operate the means of converting it into warmth. This was not easy, as coal dust burned sluggishly and the quality was poor. After a learning period, primitive stoves of bricks and metal were designed and installed in every living quarter, small or large. To get the smoke out, the Japanese set up a stovepipe manufacturing shop in the basement of the education building, and good, reliable, leakproof stovepipes were much in demand. My involvement in uncovering a black market operation in smuggled stovepipes is one of the highlight memories of my thirteenth year.

To prepare the coal dust to burn, we had to make it into balls or bricks by mixing the dust with soil and water and drying the black slurry in the sun. Unfortunately, this did not work very well on overcast winter days. If you walked around the camp on a sunny day, you would find coal balls drying outside most huts. We had a potbellied stove in the middle of our dormitory, and on winter mornings, a kind teacher from our school would light it before we got up. What a treat to get out of bed to some, if only a little, heat. It was not so comfortable at the end of the day. Getting into a cold bed in a subfreezing dorm was a nightly struggle. Each winter, I used to get chilblains on my fingers and toes. They would swell up, constantly itch, and sometimes bleed. It was a particular frustration as I was more prone to this than my peers.

TWELVE-YEAR-OLD DETECTIVES

Jimmy and I were best friends, and our personal spaces, eight feet by four feet, were next to each other in the dormitory. We each had a mattress on the floor, with all our personal possessions at its head. And the room was also our classroom.

The year was 1944. It got dark early on winter evenings, and we liked to run around in the gloaming to get warm and play games of hide-and-seek and make-believe adventure. On a late November night, we knew we were out past the time we should be, for evening prayers had started a few minutes earlier. The others would be singing a hymn and thinking of faraway parents.

Suddenly, passing nearby was a dark, crouching, and, to us, sinister figure, with a bulky bag over his shoulder. We followed as quietly as possible, and as our quarry was clearly in a hurry, we sensed that he did not know we were there. It became so dark that we thought we had lost him, but a flash of light ahead gave us direction. This is where twelve-year-old imagination fuses with reality. *He's a pirate looking for a place to bury his treasure. But no. Wait! We are Sherlock Holmes and Doctor Watson, and here is Professor Moriarty planting a trap for Scotland Yard.*

All of this was in sharp contrast to the tedium of real life, our prison life. Nothing exciting seemed to happen, and we faced the daily grind of school, our job pumping water, and the twice-daily roll calls by the guards. The days dragged on, but here, out of the blue, was real adventure.

Danger! Stay quiet. Don't even whisper, I thought. The figure cleared some bricks from a hole in a wall. What wall was it? Who lived in the hut on the other side of the wall? Such questions flooded in. The man started removing strange-looking things from his bag and pushed them through the hole. Suddenly, we recognized the shapes. They were stovepipes! Oh, how twelve-year-old boys love discovery, and to know and keep secrets. This was indeed *our* secret. Breathlessly and silently, we ran back to evening prayers, quietly slipped in, looked at each other in the faint candlelight, and smiled with a smile that wrapped itself right around our being. It was hard to get to sleep knowing something secret, and perhaps really important in the grownup world!

Next morning, during midmorning break from class—keeping our secret close to the bone—we located the wall and the hole, which by now had been bricked up. It looked so innocent in the light of day, but we knew that behind it was a dark secret. Only we knew that. There were never enough stovepipes to go around, and the result was that a number of prisoners were without effective heat in their huts. No wonder there was illegal smuggling!

It was almost too good to be true for us boys to have stumbled across the stovepipe scheme. What secret knowledge we held! There was power in that. After a time, however, we reluctantly surrendered it, for the knowledge was also a burden, and we reported our secret to the discipline committee. This was an elected board designed to maintain order and protect wrongdoers from more-serious punishments such as flogging, solitary confinement, or possibly even death by the Japanese guards. I cannot remember how the affair ended but know that the thieves were punished but not exposed to Japanese wrath.

Our reward was a can of beans which we secretly cooked on a campfire in one of the more remote corners of the camp.

Everything depended on moral authority. Our camp community had given the committee the moral authority to act on our behalf, but it could go only so far without the ability to enforce its decisions. Above all, it did not want to appeal to the higher authority: our enemy, the Japanese. Such are the difficulties of a struggling democracy within a totalitarian regime. In our open society, we cannot legislate above our own moral values. How fragile that can be in today's world.

Rat Catchers

When the problem of a growing infestation of rats in the camp became serious toward the end of the war, the commandant organized a rat-catching competition. This was taken up very seriously by us boys. The irony was that though we were the captives and the Japanese the captors, we were being asked to take their role in the rat kingdom! There would be prizes for the teams that caught the three largest rats by April 1. My best friend, Jimmy, and I took much delight in modifying an old defunct trap we had found on the scrap heap and getting it to work with a powerful spring action. This was my first engineering project.

Then we had to decide where to put it in order to catch our prize. This turned out to be more complicated than we had at first thought, as various rat-catching teams were staking out areas for their exclusive use. Quite how this worked I cannot remember, but I know we did not have a good location, so stealthily and late at night when all were asleep, we placed our trap in a dark attic area which my brother Rupert and his team had claimed for their own. So far, we had caught nothing, and the April 1 date was getting very close. Next morning, I was groping for the trap on my hands and knees in the filth and darkness. Suddenly I felt the stiff pelt of a dead rat. Instead of being repelled, I called out in delight and dragged the stiffening carcass into the daylight by its tail. We had caught a monster, eighteen inches from nose to tail!

The teams brought their trophy rats to the commandant's office for measurement and final judging. The big question was, Would ours earn a prize? Rupert's team complained that we had been in their area, but they were fortunately overruled since the trap itself was ours. We received second prize, which, once again, was a can of beans. To the two of us, in our state of perpetual hunger, the reward was highly prized and eagerly devoured. Questions remain: What happened to the trap? Did we catch any more rats? I retain only the glorious memory of winning the prize.

LONGING, GRIEF, AND DARKNESS

> *Though nothing can bring back the hour*
> *Of splendor in the grass, of glory in the flower;*
> *We will grieve not, rather find*
> *Strength in what remains behind . . .*
> *In the faith that looks through death.*
> —William Wordsworth

One winter afternoon, the headmaster of our mission boarding school requested that all six of us Hoyte children meet him in his room. I remember wondering why this would be, since we were all in different grades and involved in completely different camp activities. There were ten stone steps leading up to his second-floor room, and I counted every one. I had a sense of foreboding. What could this mean? What could have happened?

It was a small room, and we crowded in, sitting on the bed, on the one extra chair, and on the floor. "Pa" Bruce broke the news in a seemingly matter-of-fact voice. To us, it was deadpan flat with no emotion and as hard-edged as a sword. I am sure that, from his point of view, he spoke with as much compassion as he could possibly muster, but it was no use. He had just heard from our father and had to tell us that our mother had died.

We sat there in complete silence, numb and unable to take in this startling news. It seemed to come from outer space, from another reality, and thus could not be true. Did Pa Bruce pray with us? I cannot remember. Did we hug each other for mutual support and comfort? I don't think so. If our dad had been there, our response would have been entirely different. We would have clung to him for emotional and spiritual support and together faced the bleak future without a mother. But he was not here, and Pa Bruce was no substitute, being to us a rather cold, unemotional administrator of our school.

The result was that we went off into our individual lives burdened with unimaginable grief and with no support from each other or from friends or teachers. For all the closeness and mutual joy of our family in Chefoo, we were now incapable of coming together as a grieving family or of being able to express that grief to each other. Part of the problem was that the structure of the prison school meant the different grades were so separated in everyday life that we as a family spent practically no time together. We were now imprisoned at a deeper level. With no parent to bring us together, we were emotionally adrift. A darkness had set in.

One of the teachers, Gordon Martin, must have sensed something of what we each were going through. He invited us six to his hut for a meal, encouraging us to share with each other. But it was a one-time shot and only a tiny glint of light in the overwhelming darkness. Our mother had been so much the focal point of our functioning as a family that without her, the hope of being united after the war became meaningless. This made me realize that hope had become the very driving force for my survival in the camp. Now that was gone.

Many families have some dominant problem that has to be faced. It can be the divorce of the parents, drug addiction, deep disagreement between parent and child, etc. Ours was that with such incredible oneness between all eight of us during those glory days at Chefoo, the separation when Mom and Dad left for Lanchow and now the loss of Mom, without our father being present, was devastating.

For each one of us six, and for our father, here began the long journey from inner brokenness to wholeness, from darkness to light. I believe the healing power and love that I have found in Jesus Christ to be the key to my journey toward wholeness. My eldest brother, Robin, took the hardest blow. He must have felt responsible for the rest of us but now had graduated from school and moved into the single men's dorm. He was in no position to bring us together. The structures were simply not there. My elder sister, Mary, told me years later that she had cried herself to sleep for weeks, secretly hoping it was all a lie and that we would indeed see Mom at the war's end. The six of us were on different levels of grieving, but that became directed inward and so was bottled up. This related externally to our schoolmates, teachers, and other internees in that we did not express our grief and longing. There was no funeral service or any other type of closure, and I still clung to the thread of hope that the news was false.

Thirteen hundred miles away, our father was wrestling with his own grief. As superintendent of the large mission hospital in Lanchow, Kansu, he had more than a full-time job. Years earlier, he had contracted typhus and had nearly died. Now, our mother had caught the same disease. She came home one evening with flushed cheeks and dilated pupils. Why, oh why, had they been so desperately short of vaccine? By next morning, Dad had to know what she was helplessly grappling with. He nursed her day and night, sponging her every half hour or so to bring her temperature down. He watched her in anguish, knowing that if it had not been for the war, she would have been safely inoculated. But now it was too late, and his thoughts went out to us in the prison camp, so far away and so vulnerable to the grief that would follow.

So he sent the message to Pa Bruce. How painful it must have been to put the words together to make terrible sense. How the news reached us was only revealed years later. A Chinese friend of Dad's had undertaken the dangerous journey across no-man's-land, at times on foot, to carry the letter to the guard at the camp gate. It could have been shuffled off to the mail room, where thousands of unopened letters were found at the end of the war. But it reached Patrick Bruce, and so the news was brought to us.

To add to his grief, a few weeks later, a Chinese spy sent by the Japanese to discourage westerners came to the town where Dad was and claimed to have inside news of Japanese prison camps. After giving some details about the camp at Weihsien in order to establish his credibility, he told the missionaries he had just heard that the Japanese had killed all the children. What was Dad to believe? He and the others with children in the camp waited for some kind of confirmation. After time passed without any, they finally concluded that the spy was lying. Meanwhile, there was the agony of waiting with much uncertainty.

RESCUE FROM THE SKIES

August 1945 had come, and there were rumors of Allied victories at sea. The Japanese published a weekly newspaper in English that was full of propaganda. Reported Japanese victories were closer and closer to Japan, so we sensed that the war was coming to an end. Two prisoners who had escaped earlier, Arthur Hummel and Christopher Tipton, were with the Nationalist forces out in no-man's-land, and they managed to get news into camp by means of the coolies who emptied the septic tanks each week. The coolies tended to have terrible teeth, with lots of cavities into which a message on a tiny scrap of paper could be stuffed. They also tended to spit, dislodging the message so it found its way unobserved to the ground, where a prisoner in the know could get the message. This was all kept very secret so that the rest of us were out of the loop.

August 17, 1945 was clear, cloudless, and warm. We were in class that morning when the distant drone of an airplane caught our attention. As it grew louder, we perked up our ears, for very few planes ever flew over the camp, and those that did were at high altitude. Quite suddenly, the sound was so loud that we rushed to the windows and looked out. There, unbelievably, was an American bomber, a B-24, flying low over the trees, so low that we thought it might almost touch them. It climbed, circled, and came in low again. The bold American star on its flank was unmistakable; it was clearly *one of ours*. Everyone was outside waving wildly but also wondering if the Japanese would try to shoot it down. After all, as far as we knew, the war was still on. But the plane came down toward us so brazenly, so exquisitely, with such unimaginable reality. The meaning was profound: This plane was for us! It was to give us a personal message. Our little camp, out in the boonies, had been remembered. Could it be that the war was over?

The magical plane gained altitude, heading away, after passing over us three times. There was a gasp, a hint of disappointment. Someone said, *They are leaving us! One day they will come back and deliver us*, and so it seemed when an even-greater marvel took place, almost in slow motion. The plane's undercarriage opened and seven dots appeared. Now it became clear that they were seven men parachuting down toward us. And what parachutes! Their color was drab, but to us, they were in brilliant colors, the glorious colors of freedom.

How they contrasted with the shabbiness of the camp, for indeed we were drab. After all those months in captivity, most color had gone from our lives, with our clothes in tatters, devoid of color, and our food almost as colorless as it was tasteless. So I can understand why the parachutes—so important to me—appeared to my mind as in brilliant colors. The more-significant reality was that seven very real men were dangling from them. The parachutes floated down to earth at such a leisurely pace, indeed like a vision from on high, almost too wonderful to take in and all in slow motion.

Without hesitation and disregarding the danger involved, we rushed toward the main gate of the camp, burst it open, and ran out into the fields. As we passed through it, a couple of guards brought their automatic rifles into firing position, but, in obvious confusion, they slowly lowered them. Our goal was to reach the seven airmen. We prisoners were barefoot, and the ground was rough with broken glass, sometimes jagged metal, and prickly kaoliang vegetation, but we did not care. Half a mile out in a field high with kaoliang corn, our seven godlike heroes were unbuckling their parachutes. They had their rifles at the ready, preparing to fight their way into the camp if necessary, but were now taken by total surprise by this horde of ragtag, barefoot prisoners surrounding them in jubilation.

I was one of the first to reach Jimmy Moore, an alumnus from Chefoo, who had volunteered for the mission to help free his old school. His uniform was impeccable, his ruddy complexion like a god's, and just to touch his smart uniform was breathtaking. This was as close to worshipping a human being as a boy could get. Some of the adults and bigger boys carried him into camp on their shoulders, with us smaller ones tagging along.

The seven dismounted from their human chariots just inside the main gate, and their commander, Major Staiger, asked to see the Japanese commandant. A prisoner pointed to the hall where the Japanese officers had assembled. Staiger, who was only twenty-seven, drew his two revolvers and strode in to face the commandant, seated at his desk with his hands spread out in front of him.

The moment was crucial for both sides, as the commandant probably could not be sure that Japan had actually surrendered. If it had, he knew, killing the seven would make it tougher for him and his men. If their country hadn't, for him to surrender would be an extreme act of military cowardice and might lead to *hara-kiri*.

In the crucial moment, the commandant drew his samurai sword and revolver and handed them to the major. In a brilliant response, Staiger handed them back and insisted, with one of the parachutists who spoke Japanese interpreting, that they would work together in arranging relief for the camp. We who were waiting outside were relieved to see the major come out with his revolvers in their holsters and a smile on his face.

It is hard to describe the sensation of freedom that came over me. Theo and I walked out through the guard-less gate with a sense of ecstasy. I asked him, *Do you mean that we can go wherever we like?* After nearly four years in captivity it was incredible that we now had freedom. After we had first come into camp, the world beyond the walls began to shrink and become unreal. It was almost a two-dimensional stage set. Our only reality was the narrow, colorless existence of confinement. Suddenly, the outside world became not only three dimensional but had also taken on the fourth dimension of apparently infinite possibility. From grayness, we now looked on a multicolored world. Indeed, the world was our oyster. We were free.

For the next two weeks, the camp was run by the "fabulous seven." They were intelligent, reasonable, and gracious, and put up with our adulation with quiet ease.

Printed instructions that were airdropped to us said:

> *The Japanese government has surrendered. You will be evacuated by Allied forces as soon as possible. Until that time, the present supplies will be augmented by airdrop of U.S. food, clothing, and medicines. The first drop of these items will arrive within one or two hours. Do not overeat or overmedicate. Follow directions.*

Thus began the Americanization of Weihsien. On an almost daily basis, huge B-29 bombers came overhead and dropped all kinds of rich food, clothing, and other supplies. Canned peaches were my favorite food. Of course, we overate and were duly sick.

Then the news came that we would have to wait for another month, as the only way to Tsingtao on the coast was by rail, and the Communists had blown up two of the bridges. This helped us realize that although Japan had surrendered, the war between the Nationalists under Chiang Kai-shek and the Communists under Mao Zedong still was ongoing.

How that month dragged on! We were so ready to leave, to escape the drabness of the camp, that a sense of letdown was inevitable. A new team of American military men was determined to cheer us up, and every morning, we were awakened by loudspeakers booming out "Oh, What a Beautiful Morning" from the Broadway musical *Oklahoma!* A reading room was set up with American magazines. We British boys were caught up in enthusiasm for our American liberators. Then at last—and we were more than ready—the rail line was fixed.

The day for departure came. The train slowly and cautiously progressed to the coast. As we crossed the two reconstructed bridges, I looked down into the deep ravines they straddled. The temporary girders looked more like flimsy scaffolding, inadequate to my inexperienced eye, but here we were, crossing without mishap.

Though the American air force ran the interior camps such as ours at Weihsien, the British controlled Tsingtao. We were greeted at the station by a smart detachment from the Royal Navy in their impeccable, white uniforms, and the Royal Marines band from the cruiser HMS *Bermuda* played a cheerful welcome. Housing was at the famous Edgewater Mansions Hotel, every room with its balcony, view of the ocean, and private bathroom. Four of us shared one of these luxury suites and reveled in the simple pleasure of turning on a tap and actually getting instant hot and cold water. Never had we experienced such a thing. That evening, there was a showing of an American film *Babes on Swing Street*, my first movie since *Snow White* in Shanghai! I watched it with fascination. This was America! I had just turned thirteen and was ready for the American swing lifestyle.

A troopship, the USS *Geneva*, took us to Hong Kong. Everything was stainless steel: the galley, the dinner trays, the cutlery, even the bunks. The food was extremely rich and the crew very chatty, particularly to us boys. But the weather was so rough we could not enjoy much of this "affluence," and were glad to land safely.

In Hong Kong, we were to await Dad. He did not know where we were, and we did not know how he was ever going to find us. It turned out that he had many more problems than we did. It took two weeks of persistence and assurances that another doctor could take his place for him to get permission from the local mandarin to leave his position at the hospital and go to the coast.

Before him were fourteen hundred miles of a country that was still in chaos, in the middle of the Chinese civil war. Roads and bridges were bombed out, and transportation almost impossible to find. Trying to get to Chungking five hundred miles to the south, he at last got a seat on an overloaded bus that became stuck, after two weeks of hazardous travel, at a river where the bridge had been destroyed. There seemed no way forward, but several hours later, he managed to get a ride on a U.S. army truck that was being winched across to the other side.

At Chungking, things were in chaos, but with persistence and prayer, he found that the Red Cross was looking for doctors to help with the refugee situation in Shanghai. He would do anything to get to his six children, and promised to work for the Red Cross until he could find where they were. Resplendent in the uniform of a Red Cross doctor, he took the thousand-mile flight and got to work. I never found out how long he worked there, but it must have been frustrating to still not know our whereabouts. Finally, the good news of our waiting in Hong Kong came through, and he "hitchhiked" on a destroyer to meet us.

We were housed in old army barracks on Kowloon, on the mainland across from Hong Kong island, being watched over by one or two teachers who were determined to hand us over to our parents no matter how long it took. A group of us waiting teenagers had made friends with a British Warrant Officer, Charlie Tongue, who invited us to the warrant officers' mess hall, treated us to lemonade, and, wonder of wonders, took us for motorcycle rides at the deserted Kai Tak Airport. The thrill of going sixty miles an hour with the wind in my face was a new, post-war experience.

Reunion With Dad

One day, a teacher called out to me, *John, your father is here! He is over by the reception office.* My heart started to thump with memories of Chefoo but also of the huge gap of time, distance, and grief that separated us. What would he look like? Would he recognize me? Would I recognize him? Most important—is it possible that Mom could be with him? But the thought faded, as the teacher had said *Your father* and not *Your parents*, but still there was the finest thread of hope remaining.

We hugged, and I clung to him; Mom was not there. A new, huge pall of sadness engulfed my soul. A strangely new grief was overwhelming the joy of reunion.

Elizabeth was with him already, and we all went off for a walk. As we walked, hand in hand, I realized that I hardly knew him. He was a stranger to me now, and I felt the pang of being an orphan for five years. He had suffered even more grief that we, and yet it was a separate grief. I tried to put myself into his shoes, but failed miserably. With the immediacy and desire of a teen-ager, I also experienced the tug to be with Warrant Officer Tongue on his speeding motorcycle rather than walking along with this stranger.

But there was also the joy of being reunited, and the fact that the six of us were with him now for the long voyage to England and the future together. Did I distrust him for having left us in Chefoo all those years ago? I still loved him, but it was a distant love that needed to be reawakened. Deep down, I knew that he and my mother had responded to a pressing need and had acted in good faith. What I hated was the system, the missionary mentality that put "the Lord's work" before family needs, the devout phrases and prayers that glossed over the deep schism created in family after family. In the years ahead, I would have a long road of healing to walk. Each of us did.

Many years later, after I married Luci, and Dad had died at the age of ninety-four, I had some very helpful counseling about those deep hurts that had been with me for years. As a result and with a huge weight lifted off my soul, I was able to write a letter to him, forgiving him for leaving us as orphans. I believe that I have found peace and forgiveness. The light of forgiveness has flooded out the darkness of anger and bitterness.

We had to wait another two weeks before a troopship heading to England had space for us. Of course, it was free passage, with the British government paying for our travel to anywhere in the world because of our imprisonment, even to the last bus fare. Dad had considered going to New Zealand, but as we did not have any relatives there, he chose war-torn England even though conditions were much worse there.

While we were waiting, we had some good family times together. We took trips to Repulse Bay on Hong Kong island and to the Tiger Balm Park. There was dinner with a very wealthy Chinese family that lived at the top of the cable car route. On the mainland, we also visited a retreat center that had melded Christian belief and Buddhist practice. The symbol over the gate was a cross in the center of a lotus flower.

As we hiked the dusty hills beyond the center, we came across a column of soldiers marching in the opposite direction. They looked exhausted, dragging their boots, and had rundown equipment and dust-covered rifles. What struck me in particular was their complete silence. It was as if all the energy they had was being preserved for the march, and there was nothing left over. Suddenly I remembered that China was still at war. The soldiers were sweating, and their body odor was pungent. It was as if they had just lost a battle, and all they wanted was to go home. They must have been Nationalists, and were definitely in retreat. The vivid contrast of the serene lotus ponds, temples, and exquisite landscaping of the retreat center with the harsh reality of war-torn China remains vivid in my memory.

Next day, I was walking near the military base on Kowloon and stopped by a parade ground. There was shouting and vile language. On getting closer, I found a British sergeant major drilling four very senior Japanese officers. A British soldier explained that they had been important Japanese commanders in the southern Pacific. Here was this huge, muscular warrant officer yelling and screaming at the diminutive Japanese. His language was obscene and more than abusive. I found myself feeling sorry for the officers. At that moment, they were no longer symbols of the terrible separation that had led to the prison camp but were human beings, just like me, frail and vulnerable.

Our treatment at Weihsien had been relatively benign. My sense of compassion ran right across my anger at the war. Would I have felt differently if we had been treated like the prisoners on the Bataan death march? Later, we were to discover that the Japanese High Command in the Pacific was planning to kill all prisoners in early September, on the anniversary of the war's turning toward Japanese defeat. It would have been less than a month from the day that we were set free. If I had known that, would I have thought differently? I am extremely grateful that the war ended when it did. We later learned that the camp's deliverance by parachute had been urgent because of that threat by the Japanese high command.

On the troopship heading for England, I spent time with Dad and my siblings. He told us more about life in the interior, the difficult traveling both westward and back to the coast, and more about our mother. However, he found it hard to discuss her final days. His sense of loss was beyond words. He never mentioned the Japanese spy who told him we had been killed, something we found out from another missionary at his hospital years later. It must have been too painful for him, as he may well have believed it.

ENGLAND-BOUND

Back to the troopship. We boys spent time with the green berets, the commandos of the British forces that had fought in Burma. Their tales of extreme cruelty by the Japanese were numbing and hard to believe, as we had not seen that side of the war. Were these men exaggerating? Could humans be so cruel? Sadly and much later, when I was older and more mature, I was to confirm that most of this was true. Laurens van der

Post's book *The Night of the New Moon,* Laura Hillenbrand's *Unbroken,* and a more-detailed study of the history of Asia under Japanese occupation made this conclusion inescapable.

The question was raised over and over in my mind: "Why were they so cruel?" The reason for my question is that from our point of view at Weihsien, we were treated reasonably well, though with many other problems, while thousands of others were not. Having read the experts, I have come to my own conclusion that at least part of the problem was to do with how the Japanese military was structured. There was a huge gap between the officer class and enlisted men. There was pride, elitism, extreme discipline, and a sense of the devaluation of the individual soldier for the glory of the Japanese empire. Thus, the kamikaze pilots and the willingness to commit suicide rather than surrender. This expressed itself in officer-inflicted cruelty toward the privates which was then passed on to prisoners of war. Sadism became the norm.

Camp commandants seemed to have lost sight of what we in democracies treasure, the ethic that each individual is of unique and supreme value before God. Now, when I visit Japan, I am treated with great courtesy and kindness. There is no Japanese army, just a defense force. If there were an army, I would wager it would be very different from that in World War II. A democracy has been established. It took a war to make that great nation change. America also had to learn a lesson in human rights. Thousands of American citizens were imprisoned by the U.S. during that same war purely because they were of Japanese heritage. Will we be able to relearn that lesson in the twenty-first century?

The troopship went through the Suez Canal, and we were at anchor at Port Said for a couple of days. A number of us signed up to hear a famous American band in a Nissen hut out of town in the desert. It was my first experience with Big Band music, and it blew me away. I later became a great fan of Benny Goodman, Artie Shaw, and Glenn Miller, and still have their vinyl records.

I had a strange experience while at Port Said. All alone on the ship's deck, which was level with the dock, I was looking out over the harbor and the immediate dockside when an Egyptian man came up to me without boarding the ship. He was friendly, jocular, and spoke perfect English. He was wearing some exotic perfume. I found him interesting and began to like him. Then he said something that took me completely by surprise. Would I like to come with him so that he could show me the town? When I answered, *No, thank you*, he did his best to persuade me. Eventually after things began to sour, he abruptly left in a state of muffled anger. I am so glad I never went with him. Later, I wondered if this might have been a kidnap attempt? How close was I to serious danger?

As we cruised the Mediterranean and began to think of England, fear of the future came to the surface. Family-wise I felt secure. My father was with me, and I was beginning to be at peace with him after the long years of separation. However, the huge question of why Mom and Dad had left us at Chefoo, the effects of the trauma of separation, life in the Japanese camp, and the death of my mother remained unresolved. On the other hand, my five siblings were here with me, and I thought how lucky I was to have three big brothers. The whole idea of facing a completely new reality, a postwar England with school and its demands and discipline, was daunting. We had shipboard lectures on Britain to help us adapt, but they didn't seem as if they'd help. I was about to start my new life in a semi-state of misery. If there was ever a time I needed my mother, it was then. So ended my first thirteen years. England, a strange, new world, lay ahead, and with it a contrasting sense of dread and expectancy.

Red is a strong color. My China years have left indelible marks on me, but I am convinced that everything can be redeemed. Those marks may be scars but not festering wounds.

CHAPTER 2

Post-War Britain—
High School and the Army

Orange is my color here—the blending of red and yellow. These years brought the red of my experiences in the Japanese camp in China to the English mix of high school and army, a preparation for the joyful yellow of college. Its wavelength range is 597 to 620 nanometers.

To be fully alive, fully human, and completely awake is to be continually thrown out of the nest.

—Pema Chodron

FINDING A HOME

Despite the flush of victory, Britain had serious problems after World War II. It had won the war, along with the U.S. and Commonwealth countries as allies but had had to sacrifice a many of its assets to do so. Vast areas of London and other cities had been heavily bombed. The government did not have the funds for rapid rebuilding. It had spent its resources to survive the war, and now there was little left. Food was rationed and petrol (gasoline) was hard to find. There was still barbed wire on the beaches.

We ex-prisoners of war from the other side of the world could not expect an easy return to civilization. Instead of jumping out of a frying pan into the fire, we were jumping out of the fire into an uncomfortable pan. In the delightful book and movie chronicle of a twenty-year transatlantic love affair by mail, titled *84*,

Charing Cross Road, I am reminded that as late as 1949, four years after the war, rationing was still stringent. Two ounces of meat per family per week and one egg per person per month was the rule.

Our troopship arrived at Southampton on a cold afternoon in December 1945. We took the train to a darkening London. There was a chill fog over the city. Clearly we were not dressed for this cold, damp English weather, and we were eager to get to a warm home. At Victoria Street Station, our Aunt Alice met us with Grahame, one of my teen-age cousins, our first contact with Hoyte relatives in England. We began to feel that we could belong.

Because of limited space and the size of our family, we four boys and my dad went to live with Uncle Julian in Hendon, north London. Mary and Elizabeth stayed with Aunt Frances, my father's sister—"Auntie Frae"as we called her. She and Uncle Hal, a doctor with a local practice, lived in Upper Norwood, south London, so we were separated by quite a distance. Uncle Julian and Auntie May had been medical missionaries in Africa, and their five children had grown up in Northern Rhodesia, now Zambia.

Old England.

Only Henry, the youngest—my Cousin Hal—was still at home. Since we were the same age, I had an immediate pal, and both being missionary kids, we had an extra bond. He and I would go off to various railway bridges in west London and do some serious train watching. He had a complete list of serial numbers of the major steam locomotives on British Rail and kept detailed records of sightings. Our mutual interest in stamps provided an extra pleasure, he with his special African collection and mine from China. It was a jolly household, and we four were made very welcome. There was the informality of both families' being returned expats and shared jokes about trying to fit into the structured English lifestyle.

Susanna, my uncle's eldest, had recently graduated from Oxford University, was teaching English at a nearby grammar school, and was ebullient and vivacious. Dad suggested she might evaluate my academic abilities in preparation for school. I felt that I was very far behind in all the basic subjects, and my self-image was already low because of the overwhelming English culture. To my surprise, she encouraged me and said that if I studied with the right tutoring and school, I should be able to catch up within a reasonable time. In fact, it was she who suggested The Hall. Susanna was among the special people in my life who have made a huge difference through their encouragement.

I started my English education about a year behind boys of my age, entering a small, private, and excellently tutored prep school at Golder's Green. It was called "The Hall, Hampstead." One advantage of being a missionary boy, mishkid for short, was that I was able to get a scholarship. To get to school, I had to bike, but had never learned how; that was my next project. Fortunately, our road was quiet, so my wobbly first attempts were safe enough. The traffic was terrible in the Golder's Green area, as it was one of the busiest road junctions in northwest London, so I was soon dodging trucks, buses, and learning fast. In those days, no one wore a helmet. I like the fact that C.S. Lewis chose

Golder's Green as a typical, busy suburban center for the hometown of his heroine, Sarah, in the classic novel *The Great Divorce*.

The Hall School was kind to me, offering help in subjects where I was weak and giving me much-needed confidence. Our math teacher, Mr. Beardsley, taught us some clever tricks with numbers, and the subject became a delightful game. That spring, I signed up for the school boxing competition and was surprised to win the top match. Those hard times in China must have helped. I still keep the medal, a reminder of the many adjustments I was trying to make in my new life in England.

Occasionally, we visited my sisters in south London and found Uncle Hal and Auntie Frae's home much more formal and therefore forbidding. Basically, as camp survivors, we had next to no table manners and were not used to the English style of upper-middle-class living: sit-down breakfasts, coffee at 11 a.m. (called "elevenses"), noon lunch, sitting around for a long afternoon tea, and then supper. Life seemed to be made up of preparing, eating, and cleaning up after meals. There was always the right way to hold a fork, to balance a plate on a lap for tea, and to hold a teacup at the right angle. We were used to gulping down our food. Here, they would take untold time eating a delicately spread watercress sandwich, which to me was such a waste of time.

My father needed a job and a home big enough to house us all. He bought an old, prewar motorcycle with a sidecar, and thus could take three of us with him, two in the sidecar and one behind him. It was a good way to get around while the London Underground was getting post-war restructuring.

Financially, we were in a bad way. The China Inland Mission, with which he had served for thirty-two years, was a "Faith Mission." The founder, Hudson Taylor, and his team believed that if its workers were faithful to God's calling, the Lord would provide for their needs. There were no appeals for money and no return address envelopes sent to potential donors. Instead, there was prayer and faithful living—teaching and running hospitals. Material and spiritual needs were shared though field letters which would take over six weeks by boat to reach England.

This might seem irrational to the secular mind, but, in fact, it worked. This remarkable community of faith thrived. In 1940, there were over a thousand members of the mission in China without a single appeal for money—somehow all supported by donations from a network of interdenominational prayer meetings in England. We children grew up in wonderment that all this was possible.

But the other side of the coin was that there was no retirement plan. Our family was fortunate that Dad could get a small supplemental income over the years from his father's estate. Grandpa Hoyte had been a surveyor and builder in Nottingham and in his will had allocated an extra amount to his three missionary children: Auntie Florence in India, Uncle Julian in Africa, and Dad in China. This made all the difference to us.

Although he was well qualified as a physician and surgeon, Dad was out of touch with western medicine. He would need extensive medical updating courses before he could pursue his old profession, and he needed a job now! Starting from scratch and finding the right opportunity at age sixty was not going to be easy, all the more so as many other families and returned soldiers were in the same position. However, in that summer of 1946, a job did open up. The original mansion of the Barclay family, founders of Barclays Bank, in northeast London had been trashed by the military during the war but was now taken over by a Christian mission board. Dad was to be principal of a unique institute, Livingstone College, providing courses in emergency medicine for overseas workers, with room enough for all seven of us plus the students.

FINDING A MOTHER

Strangely enough, the college had an important link to our biological mother, Grace. Dad had proposed to her while they were in the U.S., on his first furlough from China back in 1921, but she turned him down and was planning on going to India as a missionary. On returning to England for an advanced medical degree, Dad was surprised to get a letter saying she was coming to England and did not know anyone but him. Would he be willing to meet her and escort her to a certain Livingstone College where she was booked to study tropical medicine for a year? He had gladly accepted, visited her several times, and began courting her. She finally said "Yes." Now he was returning to this old haunt but in a much more complicated situation with a big family to feed and house, and no Grace to be their mother.

Soon after the job became available, we went off for a summer holiday to Willesleigh, a stately old country house in Devon. During the war, it had been a haven for Londoners who wanted to get away from the bombed-out city. Now it was run by the two Drake sisters, Eileen, "Drakins" to her friends, and Margery, as a compassionate guest house. There was always a "shepherd's purse" by the front door where guests could put donations toward others who needed to stay but could not afford it. Dad had known the sisters while he was in medical school forty years earlier, and had kept in touch. Within a few weeks of our arrival in England, Dad asked Eileen to marry him, and to be mother to his six children! What a surprise for her, and what a challenge. It was amazing that she said "yes" but she did, and they were married within three months. We kids now had to get to know this complete stranger. She was a very complex personality. Now in her forties, she had never married, and for a short time had been a missionary in Algeria.

The two sisters were quite different. Margery (Auntie Madge, to us) was gentle, caring, a deeply compassionate saint of the highest order but physically fragile. I know of no one with such a profound, thoughtful, and compassionate prayer life. She had been engaged to Robert, Lawrence of Arabia's elder brother, who later went out as a medical missionary to China. She told us that whenever Lawrence, nicknamed Ned, visited the Drake home, he would insist on sleeping on the floor, preferably outside in a tent. Auntie Madge did not tell us more about those days or why the engagement broke up. Perhaps she was not physically fit to face the rigors of missionary work in China. She suffered from a number of physical ailments which she took in stride, and never complained or prevented them from allowing the radiance of her spiritual beauty to shine out.

"Drakins" to her friends and foster children, was very direct, practical, a brilliant organizer, visionary, and planner. She was also compassionate—and she had to be to be our mother—but her compassion was more hidden, and it had a hard edge. With the needs of our dysfunctional family, she was the one to make things work, to take over the huge task of running the household side of Livingstone College—feeding us all when food in Britain was strictly rationed, and getting us into shape to face the strange world of English society. Auntie Madge would never have been able to have done it, but in some ways, we felt closer to her than to our own stepmother.

Moreover, Eileen could be quite demanding, and I am sure she had to be, for she set high standards. She had the strange characteristic of being hardest on those who were closest to her. For instance, she was like a mother to the son of the financially struggling gardener at our later home in Reigate while being hard on her two stepdaughters. She could also be moody, so that we often did not know where she stood emotionally. This set the tone for family gatherings. "How is Mother today?" we asked. If she was in good spirits everything would go along swimmingly but if not, there were silences and uncertainties. Also, she would get terrible migraine headaches and lie in bed all day with the drapes pulled.

On the other hand, the circle of her love and affection was wide, as she had the gift of extending her mothering to a much wider clan than her stepchildren. Before the war, she and a friend had opened a home to children of missionaries, and some of these dear folk—our peers, Beth, Stephanie, Claire, Dennis, and others—looked to her as the mother they had lost while their own parents were abroad. As the years passed by, her more-unsettling characteristics softened, and I came to love her in a special and profound way. When Dad was in his eighties, they were like two lovebirds, and we children had grown much closer to them.

The family, now eight, moved into Livingstone College that summer. We kids had the huge, ramshackle, rundown mansion to ourselves until the autumn term started. There was room for everything, big hallways, and a huge library full of medical books (not very exciting for teen-agers.) There was even a separate room just for the Ping Pong table. There were rows and rows of glass cases with amazingly accurate models of horrendous tropical diseases for students to study, a bizarre setting for us children. It was a perfect "haunted house," with creaking back stairwells and unexplained attic noises. Everything was on its last legs and could fall apart at any moment.

Our new mother found the first few months particularly difficult, for she had to spend much time at the shops, in line, using up the family coupons to get basic food for her family of eight. Then there was the fiery-tempered cook and a dishonest charwoman who exclaimed, "Oh, I wouldn't steal from you, ma'am"when six pounds of our precious, rationed sugar were found missing.

In many ways, we were still a dysfunctional family, getting to know each of our parents and settling down to new schools. Things tended to come around full circle. My father, who was born in 1885, had been named Stanley after the explorer and journalist Sir Henry Morton Stanley, who that same year had reached David Livingstone, the famous explorer and missionary, in remote Africa. Now he was principal of Livingstone College!

He had a huge task ahead, preparing for and lecturing to thirty to forty students in an intense one-year course in hygiene and tropical medicine. He loved teaching, but preparations were exacting, and making complicated medical terms understandable to lay people was a new challenge. And in addition, he also had to administer the college with minimal staff.

FINDING A SCHOOL

Once we had moved to Livingstone College, I had to find a high school, and was fortunate enough to get admission to a well-established Public School in Epping Forest with only a hundred eighty students. Only about two miles from our new home, it was easy to get to by bike. Forest School had been founded over a hundred fifty years earlier, was just for boys, and accepted both day students and boarders. I had pretty well caught up with my studies by that fall, and found myself in the "third form."

The "Public School" system was considered the backbone of British higher education, and the oldest schools went back to the

Our family at Livingstone College with our new mother, 1948. Back: Eric, 20, Mary, 17, me, 16, Rupert, 18; Front: Robin, 22, Eileen, 49, Dad, 63, Elizabeth,14.

fourteenth century. Among the famous ones were Eton, Harrow, and Rugby (where rugby football was invented), and they were often heavily endowed by royal patronage. The term "public"in this context means "private"and "privileged,"while other secondary schools were termed "Grammar Schools."In the late '40s, it was expected that as many graduates as possible would "go up"to Oxford or Cambridge University. In a very real sense, it was an elitist system with all its faults. However, this was where the leadership of the British Empire had come from back in the nineteenth century and first part of the twentieth, and that empire had been remarkably resilient. Many leaders of Third World countries also went through this system long after the empire broke up.

But now it was 1945. The empire was in decline and England no longer had its prewar influence. The Public Schools were regrouping, getting back on track with quality teaching, tutorials, cricket in the summer, rugby football or soccer in the winter and, probably a Shakespeare play in the Michaelmas (fall) term. Forest School would have been considered "not quite"a first-class Public School. It was small, did not have a large endowment, and lacked the prestige of larger and older schools. However, for me, with my mixed-up Chinese background, it was just what I needed. The small class size and the easy access to the teachers ("masters") gave me much-needed confidence. Its location on the edge of beautiful Epping Forest in Essex but also on the fringe of London's East End (the poorest part of the city) meant that we were a healthily mixed bag of students: not many rich, some poor, some middle class, and a good smattering of international students. In my class was an Ethiopian boy related to his country's royal family. There was very little sense of being an elite school, and this was healthy.

My first experience of the beauty and mystery of the Christian faith was at Forest School. Like most Public Schools, it was linked to the Church of England and had a chapel and chaplain, the Reverend "Basher" Clegg. I joined the chapel choir and began to appreciate the rich heritage of Anglican Church music. Thomas Tallis, William Byrd, Orlando Gibbons, and other early church composers provided a doorway to the beauty of Anglican worship. This was a new way of approaching the reality of the risen Christ, different from the evangelical upbringing of the mission school. I welcomed the change without rejecting my upbringing, and ended up viewing the two ways of seeing as an enhancement rather than a point of conflict. I attended Forest School for five years, the first two as a dayboy, cycling up from Livingstone College, but the final three as a boarder after Livingstone suddenly closed.

Poor Dad! He had to start looking all over again for a position where his family of eight could fit. We prayed as a family, and out of the blue came the possibility of another position. Dad and my stepmother were asked to run a hostel, called Maxwell House, for medical students who would later go to the foreign mission field. This was in the suburb of Chislehurst, Kent, on the other side of London. Maxwell House had been the home of Sir Charles Archibald Chubb, also known as Lord Hayter, president of the world-famous security firm, Chubb Locks. He had died only a year before we moved in, at the age of ninety-eight, and the aura of elegance was still in the air. Though a definite downsize from the vast Barclay mansion of Livingstone College, it was in much better shape, and some of the elegant furniture had been left.

As we explored the crevices and cubbyholes, hoping for some surprise treasure from the days of His Lordship, we did indeed find something special, an elegant top hat! It was one of the classic, collapsible designs, and was discovered, flat and inconspicuous, far up in the corner on the top shelf of the master bedroom's wardrobe closet. Inside, emblazoned in gold, was the royal coat of arms and the maker's name: *Thos. Townsend & Co, Lime St. London*, and, to top it off, below were the golden words *EXTRA QUALITY*. It must have belonged to Lord Hayter himself, and I imagine that he had worn it when he was made a baronet by the queen.

Thus, we had a treasure from the past and a source of much fun over the years. It was a key item for annual charades and Halloween and fancy-dress parties, and was used every Christmas when the plum pudding was carried in to Christmas dinner, blazing with brandy. The bearer would always wear Lord Hayter's top hat. We four boys were the bearers, the first with the pudding and hat, the other three with tall chef's hats and aprons, proceeding with as much dignity as we could muster to the slow, solemn chant of the "Boar's Head Carol." I still have that top hat—back on the top shelf but not collecting dust— wear it each Christmas for pudding time, and keep it for other special occasions. The other family tradition that we faithfully kept was all sitting down as a family and listening to Dylan Thomas reading his *A Child's Christmas in Wales*. The rich imagery, the pranks, the snowbound, seaside village all summed up for us what family can mean at Christmas time.

Once we got settled in this elegant hostel, the medical students moved in, and we found them a delightful, fun-loving lot. They would have to take the daily train into London to the hospital where they were training, making it a long day, so when they were back at our home, they were able to let off steam. Weekends were hilarious. My parents turned out to be excellent hosts and managers with Eileen's ability to run the household, because of all her experience at Willesleigh, and my dad managing the finances and, as a retired missionary doctor, understanding the emotional ups and downs of medical students. It was a relief to the considerable appetites of all of us young people, medical students and Hoytes alike, that food rationing had been discontinued.

Now that we had moved to the other side of London, and as I was getting more and more at home at Forest School, my parents felt that I should continue there but now as a boarder. I am so grateful for that decision because in a very real sense, it was the making of me, giving me the confidence I badly needed in adjusting to English life.

We six children were great bicyclists and would go on holidays covering considerable distances, traveling from youth hostel to youth hostel for the night. Biking the two hundred fifty miles from Chislehurst to North Wales was quite manageable. Bicycling was how I traveled to school at the beginning and end of each term. I knew all the back streets of East London, and always went through the Blackwall Tunnel under the Thames. East London was a dark and dingy part of the city in those days, and the Blackwall Tunnel, well named, was the epitome of its dinginess, especially in the winter. But it was the only way to cycle from south to north without going through the center of the city. It also had to handle a great amount of trucking.

There was just a single lane in each direction, no bike lane, and the road surface just cobblestones. Every time I went through it, I felt apprehensive, but there was no other way since I needed my bike at school. The smells of East London linger in my memory with the dampness, diesel exhaust, and smog from the many coal fires that were the only means of heating most homes. The environmental cleanup of the city was well in the future. The cobblestones would glisten with the rain. Frequently, there would be continuous drizzle, and, at times, thin layers of oil and grease from the trucks made rainbow patterns, beautiful but dangerously slippery. The warm lights of Forest School or home were a welcome sight after this hazardous journey.

The examination called School Certificate (now called "O levels") was taken in the fifth form and covered a wide range of subjects, while in the sixth form, one specialized. I chose chemistry and mathematics, and threw in divinity as a minor subject. "Divinity"—what a lovely old-fashioned term for religious studies.

As a House Monitor during my first year in the sixth form, there were certain limited responsibilities, but then, as a full

Monitor in my final year, the responsibilities and privileges were awesome, or at least it seemed so to junior boys. At its best, it was a powerful system for developing leadership and maturity. At its worst, it led to horrible abuses. C.S. Lewis's description of his school days at Wyvern College showed this in more detail. Forest School was not like that.

As a monitor, I developed a very real sense of responsibility for junior boys, and remember stepping in firmly when there was a case of bullying. I never physically punished junior boys but liked the more-positive method of issuing *packets,* sections of poetry or prose that had to be memorized in forty-eight hours.

That year was also one for leadership training in the school's Officer Training Corps. Every Public School in the country had military training. Not only was this a leftover from World War II but there also were growing tensions between the USSR under a strident Kremlin and the West, and the new leadership of Britain promoted military training in high schools. Every Thursday afternoon, we put on our army uniforms and boots and trained in a number of ways. Posture was important. We had field maneuvers, rifle practice, parade ground formations, map reading, and much more. I enjoyed it, but the need to boss around the recruits was onerous. I wrote in my diary for January 19, 1950: *After lunch had corps parade. I am a sergeant now. Last term, I had the number four platoon, the recruits, but now have number three. They are very unruly. Sgt Dawson and I took them for a short march and dismissed them at 3:30. Corps is fun but I feel I have too much responsibility. Usually before Corps I dread it, but afterwards it does seem quite manageable.*

The following year, I was made captain of our boxing team and also of chess, which we took very seriously, challenging other schools to matches. As captain, I had to make all the arrangements, book a minibus for away matches, choose the chess team members, and plan for a special High Tea if it was a home meeting. We also played the masters and were able to beat them a number of times, which certainly gave our team a great boost.

During my final year, I struggled with chemistry, which was meant to be one of my majors. My mind simply seemed incapable of getting around the subject, particularly the organic part. Despite often putting in an hour or two of extra study, to escape the possibility of failure, I eventually changed my majors to physics and mathematics, and did better. The fear of failure when everything else in my life was going well weighed heavily on me. I dodged the bullet but felt its full force later in the army.

We boarders considered ourselves the elite of the school compared with the dayboys. Only boarders could take part in the annual Shakespeare play at the end of Michaelmas term, close to Christmas. I cannot think of anything that brought our small boarding school together so effectively as the annual play. One way or another, every boarder had a part to play in its production. It was, of course, an all-male cast, including the female parts, just as in Shakespeare's time.

When I returned in 2009 to give a talk, alas, there was no longer a Shakespeare play. There is something about Shakespeare that is beyond greatness. For young people to be able to live and breathe the power of these plays is to give them an indelible heritage which cannot be matched. Our annual Shakespearean event was one of the highlights of my school years. It did not matter that my parts were small. In *Macbeth*, I had one line: "The King, my Lord, is dead." I was teased for some time because of its brevity, but I could always respond that it was quite important to know that the king was dead. For me, and for all of us boarders, to actually take part in the play was what mattered.

We boarders had to put up with some spartan living! The dormitories were unheated in the winter and had no running water in the bathrooms for washing.

Drawing and sketching were my special hobbies, and I did a number of drawings of different areas of the school! I loved design and engineering drawing, and very much wanted to be a naval architect. I must have caught something of the magic of shipping during the long ocean journey from China after the war. When asked what I wanted for my birthday, I would suggest a book on ships and shipping. This led to an interview with a career counselor at the offices of the Royal Institute of Naval Architects in London. But he warned me about the career's difficulties and competition, and I went back to school crestfallen and disappointed. It was a very low point in my school life, and I identified with the sad young man on a winter journey portrayed in Brahms' *Alto Rhapsody.*

Fortunately, when I settled on the idea of an engineering degree and started to really enjoy mathematics and physics, things changed. I thought of applying to London and Cambridge Universities. One of the medical students at the Chislehurst hostel suggested that to go to Cambridge, one should apply to each of the twenty-one colleges. With determination I sent in all twenty-one application forms and was encouraged when asked to come up to Cambridge for interviews. To everyone's surprise, I was accepted by both Christ's College and St. John's College. I was thrilled. This was the greatest boost to my self-confidence imaginable, leading to discussion by the masters at school as to which was the better college. Evidently, no one within memory had been accepted simultaneously by two Cambridge colleges. I chose St. John's. However, there was one condition for acceptance that I had not met: I would have to pass Latin at the School Certificate level even though my major was science. Such was the rule in the 1950s. My struggles with Latin continued, but eventually, I passed on the third attempt. All in all, Forest School turned out to be better preparation for life than I could ever have expected, and I have few unhappy memories.

The week after I cycled home at the end of the school year, we had a family conference. The sad news was that Maxwell House, the hostel for medical students that had been our wonderful home for three years, would close in September, only a month away, so we needed to find a new home. Once again, without the capital to purchase a house or even money to rent one, we had to explore other options. I wrote in my diary: *What then? No one knows!*

FINDING A SERVICE

My diary entry was: *Thursday, September 6, 1951. Call-up day.* This was the first day of my National Service. All young men were expected to put in their two years. My brothers Robin, Eric, and Rupert were exempt because of their prison camp experience, but evidently, I was not because I had been only twelve. This seemed unfair, but, looking back, there were some valuable lessons to be learned, and now, I am grateful for those two years.

The train from Paddington Station took dozens of us eighteen- and nineteen-year-old recruits to boot camp in Oswestry, Shropshire, with the Royal Artillery. Most of us seemed to come from public schools, and so had a lot in common. It was easy to make friends and to share the same kind of jokes. Having been boarders, it was easy to adjust to the barracks rooms with their two rows of beds. However, the amount of time taken each day to get and keep our individual space and uniform as close to spotless as possible seemed an enormous waste of time. Boots had to shine so you could see your reflection in them as in a mirror. Having been prefects and monitors at school, we found this emphasis on the minor issues of life very frustrating.

Our sergeant major was a lifer, having served his regiment during World War II, and was a strict disciplinarian. He and his assistant were planting grass seed on the bare patch of ground just outside our barrack room. A new arrival looked out the window and quite innocently started to hum the popular Anglican hymn, which most of us knew from school chapel: *We plow the fields and scatter the good seed on the ground.* The rest of us picked up the tune and soon were singing the hymn in loud unison. The sergeant major was furious and came in yelling. We were struck dumb, not knowing what we had done wrong. The punishment was standing at attention for a couple of hours each weekend day. He, of course, was thinking that we were laughing at him while all the time we were enjoying a good old school sing-along. I then saw the clash of two dissonant British cultures.

Every young ex-Public School Monitor or prefect hoped to pass the War Office Selection Board examination and go into officer training. I aspired to those heights and took the intensive three-day test. The result came soon enough, and I was mortified to find that I had failed. After the initial shock and inevitable self-doubt, I went to our commanding officer in discouragement and discussed possible scenarios. I started out, *Well sir. I have failed. What do I do now?* He was remarkably encouraging. *That's an easy one! We can transfer you from the Artillery to the Royal Electrical and Mechanical Engineers (REME). After all, you are going to study engineering at Cambridge, so why not prepare the way and make your two years of National Service count for something?*

Looking back, I am convinced that being an officer in the artillery was not the best thing for me. That failure was one of the best things to happen to me, and I am grateful. But the pain did not go away, since I found that to transfer, I would have to go through boot camp all over again. This time it was to be at Blandford Camp in Dorset in the middle of one of the coldest winters England had seen in many years.

Three and a half years in a Japanese prison camp, two years in a British boarding school, and artillery boot camp would seem to be good preparation for this new experience. However, I was not in any way ready for this winter blast. I was depressed (mainly because of the examination failure), physically tired, and, behind it all, had a real crisis of faith. All the old questions that had hovered at the back of my mind now came to the fore. Where was the place of ambition in my life now that it had been shattered? Who was I anyway? What meaning could I find in life? How could evil ever be stopped? Christianity seems so dogmatic. How could it be true? Life was not fair! Why did my mother have to die in China? Why did I have to be separated from Mom forever and Dad for those five long years? All the simple answers seemed shallow. My life seemed devoid of purpose. If I had had a sense of the personal love of God in my life, it was as if it was only a memory, a very distant one.

Winter boot camp added to these woes. Blandford Camp was high up on an exposed, treeless hillside. The huts were purely utilitarian, ugly and rundown. They had been abused during the war and needed replacement. Heating was inadequate. We had night marches in the cold, and the sergeant was constantly ordering us to do unreasonable things. I had expected that boot camp for electrical engineers would be gentler than that for the artillery. But it was the opposite, and thinking back to the balmy autumn days in Oswestry, army life had seemed so much easier then. The whole army system now appeared to be pointless and a waste of time.

One event and one relationship helped make significant changes in my attitude. The event was a weekend in Plymouth visiting Aunt Isla, Uncle Percy's widow. Aunt Isla was seventy-five, spritely and cheerful. We became immediate friends, and she gave me a parting present that I treasure to this day, a set of three beautifully leather-bound books, *Milton's Poetical Works*, dated 1845. Why was that one present such a life-changer for me? Perhaps the surprise, the spontaneity, and the grace with which it was given made me experience a moment of deep joy. I mattered. I was loved. I was surprised by this joy as it was completely uncalled for. It is often the unexpected moments of grace that provide a sense of direction and meaning.

The relationship that pushed me even more toward resolution was with a fellow soldier, Len Griffiths, who saw my desperation and took the trouble to come alongside and administer grace.

Friendship, real friendship, is a remarkable thing. If romantic love ("Eros") brings two people to look at each other in a new and wonderful way, friendship love, ("Philia" in Greek), brings them to look in the same direction, to come alongside in encouragement. That is what Len did for me. He understood the hard edges of our situation, as he was in it himself, and had a clear view of the wonder, mystery, and truth of our mutual faith but went beyond that to bring me back to a quiet point of trust and peace.

Music also helped me survive. I looked back on my school choir days with gratitude. A recording of anthems sung by the Kings College Choir was the door. Orlando Gibbons, one of the great Elizabethan composers, had put Psalm 130 to music. The words and the music summed up my pain and longing in a way beyond expression.

> *Out of the depths have I called to you, O Lord;*
> *My soul waits for the Lord more than watchmen for the*
> *morning.*

That last phrase meant much to me as I had guard duty at 2 o'clock in the morning. At that time and ever since, I have found music a door to the spiritual.

On completing boot camp I was told that I would be posted to the REME training center at Arborfield, near Reading, west of London. This meant training in field telecommunications. The news came through that it was a reasonably laid-back place. I excitedly wrote to Mom and Dad and felt a growing sense of direction. The next day, we had our "passing out" parade from Blandford. The high-ranking inspecting officer paused in front of me and said to Sergeant Perry, "Very good turnout there!" I stood tall for the rest of the parade.

We went by military truck to Arborfield. It was a beautiful day and a delight to find Arborfield camp surrounded by lush green fields, dense beech woods, and a sense of welcome from nature.

My training course was not to start for another three weeks, so I spent my time doing guard duty, two hours on and four off for twenty-four hours, peeling potatoes, and working on general cleanup. My brother Rupert was at college a half-hour bike ride away, so I was able to spend time with him, his girlfriend, Chris, and their social group. One evening, we went to a university meeting where Chinese Communist students spoke. They had been sent by their government to pass on its propaganda, and were full of their country's achievements during the previous two years. At question time, we could see that they did their best to evade some direct and embarrassing questions. This was before the Cultural Revolution, so at least the incredible cruelty to the middle and upper classes had not started.

Our country's focus was more on the Soviet Union. Back at camp, we had several military exercises for defending the regiment in case Russian paratroopers landed in the vicinity. Evidently this was considered a very real threat, though not broadcast to the general public. Only we in the military were aware of it.

When my telecommunications course started at last, I enjoyed it enormously—so much so that I became an instructor afterward with the rank of lance corporal—a single stripe on the arm—and taught the introductory two-week basic electronics course for incoming recruits.

The purpose of this training was to equip radio engineers who would then go out to Malaysia. It is easy to forget that Britain had its own Vietnam! The big difference is that the Malay people were not won over to communism, and the British government wisely and eagerly gave them self-rule. My trainees would be platoon radio operators out in the jungle, not a pleasant way to spend their two years of National Service. How close I was to being sent out is unknown. Perhaps because of my Japanese prison camp experience, I was exempt. I would like to think it was because of my potential as an electronics instructor, but I will never know. I was grateful to be able to remain at Arborfield and teach when I knew that the alternative was jungle warfare. Most of my students came straight from high school and had little or no electronic knowledge. Here was a challenge, and I found that I really enjoyed teaching technical subjects. It gave me the confidence lost at boot camp, and I became adept at explaining the mysteries of ohms, amps, and volts, making them understandable through the metaphor of running water.

FINDING A HOME OF OUR OWN

The Christmas break came and went, but where was home to be? Maxwell House had been sold three months earlier, and Mom and Dad were now living in a friend's small house near Richmond Park. Our small amount of family furniture was in storage, and Dad still did not have a job. It was 1952, well over seven years since we had come from China, and we still did not have a home of our own. Mom and Dad were longing to settle down permanently but were strapped for money. From his father's estate, Dad had been able to save £3,000—£1,000 invested in England, £1,000 in the United States, and £1,000 in China. With the latter being a complete write-off, he sold his life insurance to replace it, and also had another £3,000 left to us children from grandfather's estate. The idea began to dawn on my parents that they might buy a house in the country and run it as an old people's home. That seemed a tall order, as Dad was now sixty-seven, though my stepmother was a young fifty-three and had incredible energy. It was enough to go on. This is where the miracle comes in.

Six months of searching got them nowhere. Mom was checking out a beautiful manor house on Reigate Heath, south of London, and found that it had been built about fifty years earlier by a former lord mayor of London for his invalid wife. Over the great stone fireplace in the hall, she noticed, were the Latin words: *Domine, dirige nos*—the motto of the City of London—*Lord, direct us*. Could this be a sign? Later, she told us what happened.

As I was walking down in the garden I saw a frail old lady. She was looking so worried and said 'Do you want to buy our home? They want to turn it into flats. I can't bear it to be turned into flats. I don't know what to do.' So there and then, I told her all about ourselves. How you had all come out of China with literally nothing and how my husband was too old to work. And all about our plans for an old people's home, where elderly folk could be cared for and not just institutionalized. I must have said lots more, I was so full of it all. Afterwards she went and called our estate agent to ask just how much we could afford. I do not know what she was asking for originally because it had been taken off the market as "sold." But she said that we could have it for just £6,200! I was speechless! What a miracle!

We took the bus one weekend in February to have a look at it, and were amazed at the appropriateness of Dungate Manor, for that was its name. The setting, the lovely level parquet floors (easy for wheelchairs), the spaciousness, the ample rooms, and fine detailing were to make this an incredible family home for us and eventually for up to sixteen elderly residents for the next eighteen years.

Of course, it is one thing owning such a magnificent home but quite another making it a financial success as a retirement home. This is where our mother excelled, for she and Auntie Madge had successfully run their guesthouse throughout the war. Now, she and my dad, with we six helping as best we could, set to work to make the idea a reality. It was not to be an "institution" but a loving, caring home where each resident was treated with consideration and understanding. That was not easy to achieve, but it worked, and brought joy and peace to many elderly folk. Dad was eighty-two when he flew around the world to visit those of us six who were abroad. He would tell my friends, "My wife and I run a home for elderly people," and did not consider himself in any way fitting that category. My sister Elizabeth postponed her first year of college to help, and my parents invited German girls to come to help and also to learn English. It was hard at first to get residents, and as soon as money came in, it was spent. Our bank loaned us working capital, though, and when the books were balanced at the end of the first year, we were down by just £300, not bad for a startup retirement home.

At last we now had a home of our own. It was such a beautiful home that we did not mind sharing it with our elderly guests. I would hitchhike home from my army base most weekends and pitch in with peeling potatoes, stoking the boiler, cleaning, helping in the kitchen, and dish-washing. When all the "oldies" had gone to bed—and they all retired early—we as a family would relax in the spacious drawing room or by the magnificent fireplace in the hall and imagine we were the lords and ladies of the manor. We were experiencing the different lifestyles of the BBC series "Upstairs Downstairs" at the same time. After cleaning up supper, we had to prepare a breakfast tray for each "guest" before we could relax. The trays each had a personally preferred salt-and-pepper set, elegant china, napkin in an individually selected napkin ring, egg cup, toast, and silver toast rack, etc. So the kitchen was left each evening with every spare table or shelf covered with these trays for the next morning. No wonder we needed to relax afterward.

FINDING RESOLUTION

Back at the camp at Arborfield, I now had a deeper purpose for doing well at my job. After several months of teaching basic electricity and wireless theory, I was promoted to more-advanced classes and found pleasure in trying to teach so that the students got good grades. We lance corporals began to explore new ways to be more effective at our job. It became a time of discovering new teaching techniques and introducing new scientific concepts. One memorable moment came when another instructor told me a new device called a "semiconductor" had been developed in America that might do away with vacuum tubes. The portable radios and walkie-talkies we were expecting our graduates to operate in Malaysian jungles were heavy, clunky, and temperamental. Happy would be the day they could be replaced and the entire device miniaturized. Little did I realize that in a few short years, I would land in the middle of what would become California's Silicon Valley, and that Bob Noyce, an inventor of the integrated circuit and co-founder of the Intel Corporation, would be the conductor of our local Madrigal Singers.

I had been introduced to madrigals, sixteenth-century Elizabethan and Italian songs, generally unaccompanied, while at Forest School. In England, any town of reasonable size would have madrigal singers. Sure enough, when posted to Arborfield, I found a madrigal group in the nearby village of Wokingham, a four-mile bike ride away. Every Tuesday, there was a rehearsal, and for well over a year, I found this recreational singing a refreshing contrast to army life. You might have found me in those days cycling along a quiet country lane, relaxed and singing the tenor part to Henry Constable's "Diaphenia, like the daffadowndilly."

The second required year of National Service went quickly enough. With the challenging job of teaching, weekends at home at Dungate Manor helping with the increasing number of "oldies," and a weekly encounter with music, I stopped complaining about the army.

There was one memorable vacation that introduced me to the wonder and beauty of solitude. I arranged with Jimmy Young, a close friend in the Japanese prison camp who lived in Edinburgh, to hitchhike through Scotland during two weeks off I had that May. But when I arrived in Edinburgh, I found he had become a casualty of the prison camp, having had a mental breakdown that changed him completely from the bright, adventuresome thirteen-year-old of China days. He was frighteningly quiet and could speak only in a whisper. I was bowled over with sadness, feeling as a fellow ex-prisoner that I might have been in similar straits but now had little ability to provide comfort. I thought of my own brother, Robin, who had had a mental breakdown on our return to England and was never to recover. Such casualties of war reach down into the very heart of a family.

Clearly, Jimmy was not prepared for two weeks of adventure. But instead of canceling the trip, I decided to go on my own. Little did I know how rich solitude could be, especially in the wild mountains of western Scotland. I omitted a camera and simply had my boots, backpack, sleeping bag, and sketchbook, with a bottle of India ink and a dip pen. So off I went, sketching, climbing over mountain ranges, staying in youth hostels, meeting wonderful folks at hostels and while hitchhiking.

A solo climb of Ben Nevis, the highest mountain in Great Britain, was indescribable. This was all to lead up to my moment of wonder and longing on the Isle of Skye. After a wild ten-mile ride on the back of a cattle truck, standing in half an inch of manure, I was dropped off at the youth hostel. It stood stark in the middle of a sweeping, desolate valley at the base of the Black Cuillin, an awesome, remote range of mountains. I had read about it, but to see it in person was to take my breath away. H.V. Morton, the famous British travel writer, described it as "the Ride of the Valkyries petrified in stone." The next day, I climbed the peak on the opposite side of the valley and made the sketch on the next page.

This became a time of wonder and longing, as for a full day, I reveled in the beauty of solitude and of being surrounded and clothed with its glorious mystery. C.S. Lewis describes a similar experience in his memoir *Surprised by Joy:*

> *I desired with almost sickening intensity something*
> *never to be described, and then found myself at the very*
> *same moment already falling out of that desire and*
> *wishing I were back in it. I call it Joy, which must be*

sharply distinguished both from Happiness and from Pleasure. It might also be called a particular kind of unhappiness or grief.

I echoed that sentiment as I gazed transfixed. There was a lump in my throat. The longing was almost unbearable. It pointed beyond the beauty and grandeur of the scene to the ineffable. Clearly there was something or someone greater and more satisfying than anything this world could offer, and at that moment, I knew who or what it was. It was love, and what was surprising was that it was a very personal kind of love. The creator of this overwhelming beauty touched me, could hear me and renew me. He was love. One of the wonders of solitude is the discovery that one is not alone but surrounded by grace. I was learning the difference between solitude and loneliness.

Working this out into the physical, existential moment, I was in a state of adventure, abandon, and risk, so that I had to go

The Black Cuillin Mountains. The Youth Hostel is on the right, by the river.

and climb among those ferocious peaks. That is what I did all afternoon, discovering waterfall after waterfall during the ascent and sketching ecstatically. It became steeper and more dangerous, so, after I had reached a knife-edge ridge, I eventually turned back to the hostel. The mountain brought revenge on my trespassing its sacred precincts by meeting my downhill climb with a torrential rainstorm slashing right into my face. By the time I reached shelter, I was soaked to the skin but still on a high. I had touched the rim of heaven and survived unscathed.

So ended my two years of National Service. I celebrated it with my old friend Ken Pine, who was also being "demobbed," by together seeing the recently released movie "Fantasia." Even this had a deeper meaning. Two graduates of Stanford University, David Packard and Bill Hewlett, had started a company in a garage in Palo Alto, California. Their first product was an oscillator to help with the sound effects for the filming of "Fantasia." Little did I realize that I would be working for Dave and Bill in another seven years. As one door closed, a shaft of light from a crack in another door down the hall shone across my way. Life was all about the angles and color of light.

The next three years at Cambridge University were going to make a huge difference in my life, and I was filled with expectancy. Passing the School Certificate Latin examination at last cleared the final obstacle to entry. One thing I knew: The army experience had not been wasted. It meant I could enter academia on a sure footing. The failures and hardships of those two years were to be more valuable than the pleasures. Nothing is wasted in God's economy. I was moving along from the color red to intense orange, and heading for the bright yellow of Cambridge.

CHAPTER 3

Cambridge—Exploring Hannibal's Tracks

Yellow is the color—for the joy of being a student in such an unforgettable place and for the promise of new adventure. Its wavelength range is 570 to 597 nanometers.

THE COLORFUL LIFE AT CAMBRIDGE

To some extent, student life at Cambridge was much as it had been for several hundred years. True, two world wars had rolled over the old town in the previous forty years, but the mellow Tudor buildings had stayed as beautiful as ever. Memories of ancient comings and goings, the War of the Roses, the civil war of the seventeenth century, and the footprints of the learned—Milton, Erasmus, Newton, Wilberforce, Darwin, and other greats—provided layers of history which enhanced the soft light of autumn when I went up that fall of 1953 to start my sojourn. There were my great expectations, of course, and the contrast with the strictures of army life—the uniforms, polished boots, and wasted authoritarianism—would be immediately evident. All the freedoms of St. John's College were played out before me in their wonderful colors. Instead of Nissen huts there would be five-hundred-year-old, richly carved and mellowed halls of learning, a magnificent Gothic chapel, a four-hundred-year-old library, Jacobean dining hall, "combination rooms" (common rooms), and acres of lawns and willow along the river.

If you saw the beginning scenes of the movie *Chariots of Fire*, you will remember the arrival of freshmen getting off the train and being welcomed at their college by a bowler-hatted porter. That was back in the 1920s, but not much had changed as regards arrivals. Many students still took the train from London, and enlightened colleges provided transportation from the station. My father drove me, and we parked in Chapel Court of St. John's College to find out where I was to stay for the first year. St. John's was over four hundred years old and considered one of the loveliest colleges, with the famous Bridge of Sighs over the river and sweeping lawns across the backs.

The college system at Oxford and Cambridge dates back to the twelfth and thirteenth centuries and is directly traceable to medieval monasticism. Cambridge University itself was founded in 1209, well over eight hundred years ago. There were twenty-one colleges when I arrived, and each had its own residential life, chapel, dining hall and, in fact, provided a complete community of scholars. All but two accepted only men, and the two women's colleges were on the edge of town. This has been the biggest change since the '50s. All the colleges, and now there are thirty-one, take both sexes.

What was it like fitting into a four-hundred-year-old tradition? There were not many requirements, but the most distinctive academically was that every week, I had to see my tutor for personal instruction and review. Indeed, this was a privilege: to sit down with a professor, sometimes of world renown, for an hour and be able to ask significant questions. My roommate had as tutor the famous Sir Fred Hoyle who had revised the cosmological theory of a steady state universe in 1948. Wow! By this means it became easy for our tutors to see who was working hard at his studies and who was not. It also meant the need for only one examination a year, in June.

Somehow examinations did not seem to rate as *that* important in our lives. It was more about living the life of the college, learning to think through a matter rather than memorize a set of functions. I was expected to attend dinner in Hall each evening, wearing my gown, and to always have it on after sundown. This was a black outer garment about four feet long with slots for jacket sleeves. Graduate students wore longer gowns, almost to the ground. Arts students were expected to wear them to lectures, and we all wore them to Great Saint Mary's, the university's Anglican church, and to the university library. Gowns tended to look quite respectable during the freshman year, but by the time of graduation, they might be in tatters.

Then there was the whole matter of religious belief at Cambridge. I was a member of the Christian Union, a student society numbering about one in ten. We considered our Christian faith an important aspect of community life. The "Hyde Park Corner" of the university was a grassy patch between the Mill Pub and the river. Anyone could stand on a soapbox and proclaim his views: anarchist, communist, fascist, liberal, conservative, or religious. We were part of that conversation of a spring Sunday afternoon, and would get lively discussions going. The Union invited Billy Graham to come up, and found him well received, filling Great Saint Mary's church each evening for a week. Most members tended to be evangelical Anglicans, and a popular outreach was to cycle out to the Methodist or Baptist churches in the countryside to preach or help out if their pastor was not available.

Rather than depend on the city police, the day-to-day administration of university discipline was in the hands of the proctors. These two officials, usually members of the faculty, were elected for a year by the regents of each college. Each proctor wore academic dress, the hood of his degree, and bands. He was attended by two constables, or "bulldogs" as they were called by the students, who were college servants selected, so tradition has it, for their sprinting abilities. They wore full morning dress and top hats when on duty. These three "prowlers" could be seen on dark nights, treading the streets, bent on their policing business, out to fine us undergraduates six shillings and six pence for not wearing a gown or worse. In general terms, as a student, I was expected not to do anything *cruel, dangerous, liable to produce gambling, inconsistent with gentlemanly behavior, detrimental to good order, or violating the canons of morality and decorum.* The wording of this old tradition, dating back hundreds of years, was still in vogue.

I have a book titled *The Night Climbers of Cambridge* about the famous and sometimes infamous climbs into and over the colleges, usually at night. The monastic seclusion into which a college drew itself at night began at ten o'clock with the closing of the gates. The porter went to bed at midnight, and to enter after ten would require a *late leave* signed by the dean or tutor. Some colleges even fined those who arrived between ten and twelve. Thus began the art of *climbing into college*. After some late night outing, I successfully managed to climb into St. John's a little after midnight, but in the process managed to jab my right knee on one of the revolving spikes which was precisely designed to deter such late nighters. It took three weeks to heal, and I made my confession to the college nurse who bandaged it up with care and a smile. It was a risky but certainly a feasible way of getting back to our rooms. In my second year, a famous notice put up in the undergraduate combination room read:

> *The Midnight Rule:*
> *The rule that Undergraduates must be in college by midnight has for some time been flagrantly and persistently broken by climbing into college; in one much used place with damage to a costly copper roof. THIS MUST CEASE! The night porters will be vigilant in this matter, and fair warning is given that "He that cometh not by the door into the sheepfold but climbeth up some other way" will, if apprehended, find himself in a position from which all temptation to repeat the offense has been removed.*
> *Signed: J.S. Bezzant: Dean of College.*

I knew the dean well and appreciated his use of Holy Scripture. The warning, couched in such amiable terms, was not easily forgotten. Having spent some time dealing with these ancient and modern traditions and rules, I still find it hard to say what I found to be the mystique of Cambridge University. Was it the ancient buildings? Was it the collegiate lifestyle? Was it the fact that for over eight hundred years, students and faculty have been wrestling with ideas, debating issues, worshiping in beautiful settings, making discoveries, and creating new concepts? It certainly created an environment for imaginative thinking and spontaneity. Part of this was the simple fact that we did not have to worry about midterm and end-of-term exams, as is the case in most universities. The story of Crick and Watson and the discovery of the DNA double helix is an example of the laid-back social climate and imaginatively fertile atmosphere that the university generated.

There was also the spirit of adventure. Students seemed to delight in thinking *outside the box*. When we set out in 1956 to find Hannibal's route over the Alps, there were over twenty other expeditions that summer from the university, some financed by colleges and some self-financed. A team of students from Oxford and another from Cambridge raced each other overland by Land Rover from Paris to Singapore. With their successful journey, a book was published: *First Overland: The story of the Oxford and Cambridge Far East Expedition.*

Then there was the mystique of humor and satire. What was it about our university that enabled it to laugh at itself and then at the world? During my second year, I got to know a very unusual fellow member of St. John's by the name of Jonathan Miller. Unkempt red hair, unusual gait, a gown that was almost completely in tatters but a gifted comedian! The university comedy theater was called the Cambridge Footlights, and he became one of its stars. Peter Cook, another undergraduate, was also a member, and they began to make a name for themselves over the next few years. It wasn't long before Dudley Moore and Alan Bennett from Oxford joined them to form what became the famous Beyond the Fringe group, providing brilliant satire in London and eventually on Broadway.

Jonathan eventually became a medical doctor and directed operas at Covent Gardens in London. This talent paved the way for an even more illustrious group that had its roots in Cambridge. John Cleese and Graham Chapman were undergraduates who flourished at the Footlights and eventually formed Monty Python and the Flying Circus with Eric Idle, Terry Gilliam, and Michael Palin. I still ask myself what it was that created the whimsical environment to produce a Jonathan Miller, a John Cleese, or a Graham Chapman. And then I come upon that famous quote by Charles Darwin: "No pursuit at Cambridge was followed with nearly so much eagerness or gave me so much pleasure as collecting beetles." (*Life and Letters*, 1887).

The Birth of an Expedition

The end of the Lenten Term was in sight when on one chilly spring evening in March 1956, three undergraduate students could be seen talking excitedly as they crossed the court by the dining hall of St. John's College. Their tattered gowns flapped in the wind and, unwilling to study, they suggested coffee in rooms over the Bridge of Sighs. They slammed the door behind them, and someone wedged his gown under it to reduce the draft. The gas fire was lit and coffee put on in the kitchenette.

Their discussion concerned a notice recently put up on the screens outside the dining hall and perused on their way out that evening. Travel scholarships were to be awarded to members of the college, and to have the exciting word "travel" next to such an academic word as "scholarship" was not to be ignored! "Who gets these kinds of scholarships anyway?" and "Why can't we have a bash?" were the first questions to be asked and discussed.

What was clearly needed was a bright and original idea, but ideas seemed slow in coming, at least to start with.

However, it had been a reasonable dinner that evening, and someone had actually remembered to buy chocolate biscuits to go with the coffee, so possible plans started to be verbalized. Alas, each brilliant idea seemed to be squashed by the two who had not thought of it. But they all knew this would be their last long vacation before graduation and the need to get a job in the *real world*. Here was the last chance to have a really reasonably long holiday before work might limit an annual vacation to only two weeks. *We have got to think of something really original* led to a time of thoughtful silence.

Deep-sea diving in the Mediterranean to look for sunken treasure was out. So was a proposed trip to Tibet to look for the mysterious snow leopard. There simply was not enough money in the kitty for *high adventure*. Someone broke the stony silence with *How about Hannibal's trip over the Alps?* Another exclaimed *Of course, we would have to take elephants*! and invited a few derisive *Ha, ha's*. But a seed had been planted, and the idea began to rumble around in the imaginations of the three. However, there was no clear way of knowing what to do with it. It was getting late, and the thought of end-of-year exams dampened any hint of further imaginative thinking. A scuffle for gowns, the turning out of the gas fire, and general movement toward the door indicated that the future Cambridge Hannibal Expedition was on the move, but alas, as yet only to bed.

The idea lay dormant for at least a month but was awakened by an unusually heated discussion between two gentlemen of note, Sir Gavin de Beer, curator of the Natural History Museum in London, and Dr. Arthur McDonald, professor of classics and senior tutor at Clare College, Cambridge. They were having an intellectual argument, a *philological sparring match,* and were using the media to make their points. The intense debate concerned Roman and Carthaginian history, topography, toponymy, philology, geology, zoology, astronomy, and climate change. The issue was the question, "Which way did Hannibal and his army cross the Alps?" The London *Times* and BBC television and radio picked up the story. Everyone knew that Hannibal, the famous general from Carthage, and his army of thirty thousand men—with their thirty-seven war elephants helping terrorize their foes in battle—had crossed the Alps in 218 B.C. to defeat Rome, but the question of which way he'd gone had remained one of the classic mysteries of history. Sir Gavin had just come out with his book *Alps and Elephants* and was adamant for a southern route over the Col de la Traversette. Dr. McDonald countered with a strong argument for a more northerly pass, the Col de Clapier.

What fascinated the undergraduate students, and a wide swath of the general public, was that it really did not matter which *way* Hannibal went. That he had gotten over the Alps with his army and nearly defeated Rome was one of the great turning points of history. However, the mystery of his route remains and over the last two thousand years or more, scholars, generals (including Napoleon), and historians have puzzled over the evidence and come up with differing conclusions. The challenge was to solve one of history's greatest mysteries. There were clues from two sources: first, the history books, primarily the record of Polybius, the brilliant Greek tutor to Scipio Africanus's children; and second, the Alps themselves, where landslides and weathering have affected the topography and place names had changed over the last two thousand years.

I was one of those three students having coffee over the Bridge of Sighs, and now that we knew of this debate, we began to think that it might indeed lead to a worthwhile summer expedition. The idea would be to travel the Alps, hike over the possible passes that Hannibal could have taken, and compare what we found with the classical texts. To confirm the idea, we thought it might be good to present it to Dr. McDonald, just down the street at Clare College.

The phone rings. "Hello. Is that Dr. McDonald? This is John Hoyte of St. John's. Three of us students have been following your famous debate over Hannibal's route and have an idea which we would like to present to you. Would you be available for lunch at the Arts Rooftop Cafe?"

It was as easy as that, and before we knew it, we were conversing with the great man himself. Not only was he a gracious and generous listener but he also encouraged us to go ahead with the idea of a Cambridge expedition. This was the moment to strike. Next day, we submitted our application for the university grant towards financing the "Cambridge Hannibal Expedition," and just got it in on time. Two weeks later, we heard that we had been awarded a grant of twenty pounds, about $180 in value today. The expedition was launched.

The battle royal over Hannibal's route was certainly raging at a high academic level in England. Sir Gavin had made his first lunge with his *Alps and Elephants*. Dr. McDonald replied with a straight-to-the-heart stab in *The Alpine Journal*. Sir Gavin's riposte was his television program produced by the BBC which seemed to have won over a lot of the public in Britain. Dr. McDonald stuck to his unassailable *marching times* argument and the need for a definitive view of the Po valley.

And here we undergraduates had landed right in the middle of it all. None of us were classicists, but we all loved history and mountaineering. And I have always had a love for elephants.

A BRIEF LOOK AT HISTORY

Hannibal and his army came from Spain. Although Carthage, his home base and power center, was in North Africa, the city-state's major colony was at Carthagina in southern Spain. When it lost the first Punic War (264-241 B.C.) against Rome, heavy disarmament was imposed, including the destruction of its elephant stables. Hannibal, the new, young leader, aged twenty-six, had energized the prospering colony in Spain—in theory to pay off war reparations but in practice to form an army to destroy Rome. It was there that he developed his secret plan to attack Rome by land, since Carthage had lost its sea power, and built up a formidable army of thirty thousand men, thirty-seven elephants, and several hundred cavalry. He set off in 218 B.C. and was determined to reach and destroy Rome, whatever the cost.

The coast route to Italy that would bypass the Alps was heavily guarded by Rome and considered impassable. But before Hannibal ever reached the mountains, he faced a major challenge in getting his army and elephants over the fast-flowing Rhône in what is now France. This was his first serious difficulty, as his passage over the Pyrenees from Spain to Gaul was relatively easy. The elephants crossed the Rhône on towed rafts. Several went overboard, and their mahouts were drowned, but they managed to get to the eastern shore using their trunks as snorkels!

Polybius told us that Hannibal took nine days from his first encounter with the Alps to reach the summit pass, so one of our challenges was finding the nine-day stretch that would best fit Polybius's account.

Hannibal and his army eventually reached the summit pass, having been heavily attacked by Celtic tribes and caught in a snowstorm. Even astronomy was part of our mix of information! At the time of the crossing, the Pleiades, a very distinctive constellation, was setting over the horizon. Calculating back to 218

Sir Gavin de Beer and Dr. Arthur McDonald fighting it out.

B.C., we found that the crossing must have taken place in late October. At the summit, Hannibal gave his exhausted men two days to recover before making his famous speech of encouragement and starting the precipitous descent. This took at least two days because of the steepness and a rock formation that blocked the elephants. Once his force was down on the plain of the Po River, Hannibal captured the capital of the Turini tribe—modern-day Turin—and proceeded to defeat Roman armies in four great battles. The final one, at Cannae southeast of Rome, was an utter catastrophe for the Romans and raises the question of *Why didn't he then capture Rome?* History still hasn't come up with a good explanation, although Hollywood, in its eternally romanticized view of the past, decided at one point that the love of a woman was responsible.

After fifteen years on the Italian peninsula without ever quite winning victory, Hannibal and his faithful army left for Carthage by sea and faced Scipio Africanus at the battle of Zama, near Carthage. This was Hannibal's only defeat in battle, and he spent the rest of his life as a consultant general to various kingdoms in the eastern Mediterranean.

THE CAMBRIDGE HANNIBAL EXPEDITION

As we students became further involved with the history of Hannibal, things got more and more interesting. A visit to the British Museum proved a gold mine, allowing us to handle coins that had been minted by Hannibal's army during the long march from Spain through Gaul into Italy. Today, if you walk into the British Museum, everything of interest is strictly under glass. But not then, though security was strict. Having had the great doors slammed and locked firmly behind us, we had to sign special forms in an anteroom. Then we were shown to a long, low table, and the precious coins were brought out on quaint wooden trays.

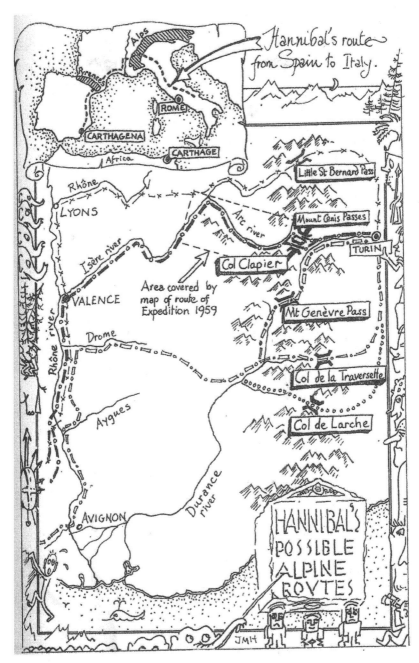

Which way across the Alps—for Hannibal, for us?

The priceless ancient coins had clear images of elephants, both Indian and African. Holding them brought a moment of unexpected surprise and joy, a revelatory instant of identification with that famous journey over two thousand years ago. Somehow I felt drawn into the action in a new way, as if some magic power had taken me under its spell. Here were touchable, polished surfaces, worn edges—the real thing—and I might even sense the fragrance of living history. The coins clinched the deal. We were now fully committed to the serious quest of finding Hannibal's actual route through the Alps and to telling its true story.

As we studied our maps, it became clear that there were five Alpine passes that should be considered for Hannibal's route: the Little St. Bernard, the Col de Mont Cenis, the Col de Clapier, the Col de Mont Genevre, and the Col de la Traversette. The American adventurer Richard Halliburton had taken an elephant over the Great St. Bernard pass in the 1930s. However, his best-selling book of travel adventures made clear that he hadn't done his homework. Without studying Polybius or the terrain, Halliburton chose the Great St. Bernard Pass because it made a good story, integrating the famous monastery and St. Bernard dogs, and he admits it.

For our part, we wanted to be as thorough as possible. Whichever pass we chose had to provide an expansive view of the Po valley and have room at the summit where thirty thousand to forty thousand men could camp. Also, the descent had to be dangerously steep. The Little St. Bernard Pass didn't match up on either count, and the Great St. Bernard Pass lay too far north to be considered. We agreed that the Col de Mont Cenis and the Col de Clapier should really be the focus of our research expedition, although we would remain open to Sir Gavin's arguments for Traversette. On the way south toward Italy, we could also look at the pass of Mont Genevre, as a main road went right over it.

Meanwhile, we would all read Polybius's history and get back to the British Museum, immersing ourselves further into the ancient world. Indeed, a second full day there helped us mentally acclimate to the culture of mighty Carthage, gazing at its carvings and scripts and speculating on the life of the great enemy of Rome.

Finally we were ready to take off for the summer's expedition. Ours was strictly a low-budget affair, hitchhiking, staying at youth hostels or camping, and hiking over the mountain passes. Everything we needed—sleeping bags, bare essentials, towels, etc.—had to fit into our rucksacks. We did not carry a tent, hoping to sleep under the stars or in a barn if a hostel was not available. Dorothy Smiley, a ninety-year-old resident at Dungate Manor, stitched a flag for us with a Union Jack and an elephant rampant which we held as we posed for a photo for the *Daily Telegraph*. She was thrilled to see it in the paper the next day.

Happily, the Cambridge Hannibal Expedition of 1956 was a success at every level. The weather was kind, and we were able to reach each night's destination, usually a youth hostel, without any problems. The '50s were great for hitchhiking, and the Union Jack attached to our rucksacks brought friendly drivers to give us lifts. The final hitchhike, on a powerful oil tanker chugging up the Rhône, gave us good views of the probable spot for Hannibal's crossing and of the "island," where his army had left the river and headed for the mountains. We were able to climb the two major passes that had the best claims to being Hannibal's: the Col de Clapier in the northern Alps and the Col de la Traversette in the south.

Making our efforts as scientific as possible, we drew up a spreadsheet listing the nine specifics that Polybius gives for Hannibal's pass. We then awarded up to five points to the ones that met the conditions. Our conclusion was that out of a total of forty-five points for a perfect match, the Col de Clapier got forty-two, the Col de Mont Cenis thirty-three, and the Col de Traversette only twenty-six, since it gave no view of the Po valley, had no space near or at the pass for an army of thousands to camp, and did not lead down to the Turini capital. We knew that Sir Gavin would not like our conclusions but felt sure enough of them to challenge him to a debate on BBC. Unfortunately, he declined to accept the offer. It would have been a great feature, with maps, photos, and personal stories.

We also took pictures from several passes, looking for good views of the Po valley. The view from the Col de Mont Cenis was minimal, though this was a very definite requirement for Hannibal's pass as outlined by Polybius, but the route had several other points going for it. It was the one Napoleon had taken when he invaded Italy, and, picturing himself as another Hannibal, he claimed it to be the right one.

Back in England, we gave the Robertson Travel Fund of Cambridge a full report of our findings, including detailed charts and photos. I am sure there were no complaints as to how the grant had been spent. Richard Jolly, my co-leader of the expedition, submitted an article about our adventures to the *Manchester Guardian*. I received this cryptic note from him a few days later: "No comment, kid! *Guardian* sent it back, said it fell

The Cambridge Hannibal Expedition takes off. From left, Richard, Elizabeth, me, and David.

between two stools and they weren't interested. I did not change it but sent it to a higher class paper and . . . read your *Times*, boy!"

Off I went to buy a copy of the London *Times* and there it was, three full columns titled "Cambridge Carthaginians."

It was a masterly piece of work, flowing nicely from the academic to the whimsical. Richard described Sir Gavin's arguments for Traversette with generosity but ultimately showed their weaknesses by citing what we found on the ground.

Apart from our love of adventure and the quest for Hannibal's route, our other and greatest asset was the deep spiritual bond shared by Richard, my sister Elizabeth, and myself. This gave an added dimension to the team. We overcame the difficulties and challenges together, leading to a deepening sense of unity and trust—so much so that it was achingly hard to say good-bye at the end.

Looking back, I now realize how important our exploratory trip was. If we had not completed it and thought through the implications, we would never have been able to consider taking an elephant over the Alps three years later. The Yellow of college had prepared me for the Green of the Alps with its high adventure.

CHAPTER 4

An Alpine Journey—With Jumbo

Green is the color—for the rich greens of nature, for the deep woods of the Alps. It fits happily and cheerfully between blue and yellow. How much of each determines the varied shades of green, reflecting the many moods of our elephant expedition: the emotional highs and lows, the dangers, and the bliss. Its wavelength range is 497 to 570 nanometers.

Forward, you madman, and hurry over those horrid Alps so that you may become the delight of Schoolboys.

—Juvenal, *Satire* X, A.D. 200

THE GIFT OF AN ELEPHANT

By September 1958, a little over two years after our initial Cambridge expedition, none of us were thinking of the Hannibal debate. The big write-up in the London *Times* had been more than we hoped for. But now, there were just sweet memories. I was a graduate apprentice at Joseph Lucas Inc., an engine manufacturer in Birmingham. I was staying at the downtown YMCA. Joe, a friend also staying there, was interested in planning a climb in the Alps. One evening, I sat down with him and shared the slides and scrapbook of our trip. Joe whimsically asked, "Why don't you take an elephant?"

I laughed as I recounted all the reasons it would be impossible: no money; no elephant; no experience; no reason to justify it; no possibility; no way. But the question lodged in my mind, and I could not get to sleep that night. I began to imagine the possibilities. What if I were able to get an elephant? I started to think in terms of *we* instead of I, for Richard, my best friend at Cambridge, would have to be involved if anything as challenging as this were to work. We shared a similar crazy imagination, and had already climbed Hannibal's possible passes together.

What kind of elephant? It would certainly have to be Indian, as African ones were hard to tame and notoriously unreliable. A comforting thought injected itself as I was remembered that the British Museum had shown us Carthaginian coins with both Indian and African elephants. What about a team? How about equipment? We would need insurance. My mind shut down as I considered the enormous costs involved. I eventually got to sleep.

The next day was another workday. My evening was free, so I got out my portable typewriter and put together three letters, to the British consuls in Geneva, Switzerland, Lyon, France, and Turin, Italy—the closest major cities to the Col de Clapier. My request was simple: Would they happen to know anyone who might have an elephant available for a British expedition over the Alps following Hannibal's route? Of course, I couldn't write as a poor engineering apprentice from the Midlands of England. With sheer audacity, I wrote representing a new entity: the British Alpine Hannibal Expedition.

There was very little chance of anything in return beyond a courteous or whimsical letter from one of Her Majesty's Consuls General, though I did wonder what kind of responses I might receive.

A week later, I was waiting in line for buffet supper at the YMCA, in possession of a long envelope from Turin that I had just picked up from the mail room. The line was moving slowly, so there was time to open it, revealing the Royal Coat of Arms and the letterhead "British Consulate, Turin." It read:

> *Sir: Unusual as your request may be—well, unusual,*
> *I should perhaps say, for a Consulate—I am happy to*
> *inform you that I have been able to secure the offer of*
> *an elephant for your projected crossing of the Alps next*
> *summer.*

My eyes grew wide as I read and reread the letter. It went on to say that on the very day my letter had arrived, *La Stampa*, the local newspaper, mentioned a particularly energetic young elephant at the Turin Zoo. Thereupon, Mr. Bateman, the consul general, called the zoo, reaching Arduino Terni, the managing director. "Would you have an elephant available," Bateman asked him, "for a British expedition over the Alps following Hannibal?" Sight unseen and quite incredibly, not only was the response positive but Signor Terni also offered to provide the elephant free of charge. He may have thought of this as good publicity, but the sheer generosity of the act overwhelmed me. Signor Terni had two requests: that we have the elephant insured and that the crossing be in the summer rather than in the fall when Hannibal crossed.

Imagining Jumbo, our elephant, striding along with our group as we crossed the Alps was difficult for me, but there it was. I had an elephant for a new expedition. The greatest hurdle of all, finances, seemed magically to have disappeared, since the addition of Jumbo could be expected to generate sponsorships and other income from newspaper and magazine publicity. But the next day, the reality of the offer began to sink in. Then came the doubts.

An expedition would attract international interest. Was I capable of organizing and running an expedition of this magnitude? I had never led an expedition of any size, let alone one with this potential. The Cambridge climb had been an exploration by four like-minded friends. None of us had been the leader. Now the team, whoever would be in it, would need real leadership. There would be huge risks. What would be involved in the planning? How could I put together a cohesive, congenial team in the few short months before summer? Would Richard be available to help me? These questions all seemed unanswerable, but with an offer like that, how could I refuse to try? This was the time to put aside doubts and go forward with confidence. Richard, in far-off Kenya, wrote that he would be available.

As soon as he returned to England, Richard and I sat down and drew up a list of the needs and responsibilities. It was formidable in length: leader, secretary, treasurer, publicity officer, literary expert (to refer to the original Greek if necessary en route), archaeologist, veterinary officer, linguist fluent in French and Italian, photographer, quartermaster, doctor, and cook. We had to be very selective.

Since everything was going to revolve around Jumbo, a good veterinary officer was a must. Richard asked the advice of Professor Pugh, head of the Cambridge Veterinary School, who, thinking a graduate student might be persuaded to come along, suggested that Professor Hickman might have some ideas. Hickman had had extensive experiences with Indian elephants during the Burma campaign of World War II, and had been in charge of transporting a number of elephants from Germany to Holland after the war.

Pugh immediately picked up the phone and dialed his colleague. When asked if he knew anyone interested in going on the expedition with an elephant, Hickman spontaneously answered that he would go himself. Thus, the expedition had a veterinary officer of the highest order. By the middle of June 1959, our team had taken shape:

The expedition team, ready to go. From left: John Hickman, Jumbo, Ernesto, Jimmy, me, Clare, Cynthia, Richard, Michael, and Baldi.

John Hoyte: leader and publicity officer
Richard Jolly: secretary and leader of the daily advance guard
Professor John Hickman: veterinarian
Cynthia Pilkington: treasurer, linguist, and cook
Jimmy Song: photographer
Michael Hetherington: quartermaster and classicist
Clare Harden-Smith: cook and assistant quartermaster
Baldi: our truck driver, provided through the generosity of Signor Terni at the zoo
Ernesto Gobold: mahout

John Hickman was our senior statesman, and we depended on him for wise advice in difficult situations and in particular when Jumbo's health was involved. Cynthia, a friend of Richard's from Homerton College, Cambridge, had traveled extensively and was fluent in French and Italian. She would be an ideal treasurer, dealing with British, French, and Italian currency. My sister Elizabeth could not come, as she was heading to Singapore for mission training in the Far East. But her friend Jimmy Song, an experienced photographer, took her place. Michael Hetherington, a good friend of mine from St. John's College, was our classicist. He could read Polybius from the original text, and was also a perfect quartermaster, taking care of our supplies and provisions with his quiet, assuring nature. Clare Harden-Smith was a close friend of Elizabeth's and mine who was about to go on a post-graduate zoology scholarship to the United States. She loved horses, and the prospect of riding an elephant over the Alps may have seemed for her a logical extension. She would be our cook; her *joie de vivre* and practicality were great assets. Finally, there was Ernesto, who was hired by Signor Terni and handled crises with calm and inner strength. We could not have had a better mahout for Jumbo.

Of course, the final and most important member of the team was our elephant. Richard and I felt it imperative that we get acquainted with her well before the planned start of the journey. We set off with little time to spare, over the Channel by ferry, then by car across France and into Italy to rendezvous with our elephant at the Turin zoo. Signor Terni warmly welcomed us and walked us over to the elephant stables. There was Ernesto talking quietly to Jumbo. We immediately liked Ernesto and made our acquaintance with his charge by offering sugar lumps and apples. It was a success. She liked us.

Richard and I wanted to call her *Hannibella* (*Bella* for short) but were overruled since she only responded to *Jumbo*. So it was, although the press was to get good mileage from her alternative name of *Hannibella* during the expedition. Next day, we set out with Ernesto on a field expedition on Mount Superga, above Turin, to test how our elephant would climb at various gradients. Once again, a great success. She was agile, limber, and could handle steep gradients with ease.

And there was a new discovery! When the gradient was uncomfortably steep, she would start climbing on her front knees.

Ernesto assured us he would take Jumbo out for regular exercise until the expedition began. We left Turin feeling very pleased with the trip and hurried back to England with a new idea: elephant kneepads! Since Lotus Ltd., which was famous for its women's shoe fashions, was already making elephant boots for Jumbo at no charge we added the kneepads to our request.

In June, we invited the team to a weekend at Cambridge to get to know each other, settle organizational matters, and clarify academic questions. Richard and I presented the case for the Clapier route as clearly as we could, and left the others to make up their minds. We were going on a quest, not simply a journey of verification; it was important that those who had not already been over the Alps should form their own opinions, which we hoped would agree. We went over the classical sources, including Polybius and Livy, the later Roman historian, as well as academic journals.

We summarized our aims in a statement:

> *We must all clearly realize that smooth organization, while vitally important, is insufficient to ensure success in presenting our message. Jumbo will sell herself. Our part is to make the background of equal interest and get across to the public and media, through our sponsors, the real question of Hannibal's route. Our approach needs thought and preparation, not that we know all the answers but appreciate which questions matter.*

Our team was now not only fully fitted for the individual jobs but also equipped for classical argument. Most of our personal camping equipment was provided free through sponsors like *Life* magazine and London's *News-Chronicle* newspaper, including mountain jackets from the company that had equipped the British Everest expedition for its triumphant 1953 climb.

Two final questions had to be answered: How would we handle the money the expedition would bring in through the ever-growing publicity and contracts with the press? Who would we invite for the ribbon-cutting ceremony to send us off? The answers were linked and led us to Princess Grace of Monaco.

The team unanimously decided that any money made from the expedition should be given to a worthy cause. As 1959 was World Refugee Year, this was our natural choice, which led to correspondence with Princess Grace, a supporter of World Refugee Year. Our plan was that she launch the expedition on its behalf at the starting point in France.

Princess Grace expressed interest in our journey and its connection to the World Refugee Year. She invited me to visit her in Monaco to discuss our plans. On arrival by train from Paris, I booked into the Hotel Hermitage, one of the elegant old hotels near the waterfront with its famous Gustave Eiffel dome. Unpacking my suitcase, I checked that I had brought everything to show the princess that might illustrate our plans: detailed maps, a picture of Jumbo, views of Hannibal's possible passes, information on the World Refugee Year, and more.

The next morning was flooded with Riviera sunshine. Everything conspired to make this a perfect day. As the clock tower over the palace portal struck nine, I walked up to the guard by his elegant pillbox and said I had an appointment to visit "Her Serene Highness, Princess Grace." He disappeared into the guardroom and soon reappeared, pointing me to a side entrance where I would be met. I maneuvered through a crowd of tourists milling around and headed for what seemed like an insignificant door to the side of the grand entrance.

An elegantly dressed woman met me there and introduced herself as Phyllis Blum, secretary to the princess. We walked through a courtyard and down thickly carpeted corridors to an elegant reception room. I sat on the edge of a Louis XIV settee and admired a Rembrandt, a Vermeer, and the other paintings. I wanted to look more closely but stayed seated as I was expecting the princess at any moment.

When she entered, I was immediately struck by how beautiful and how petite she was. Soon we were poring over maps and discussing expedition details. Princess Grace was informal and warm. She was knowledgeable about the Alps and Hannibal, and put me completely at ease. She had already been involved in helping refugee children from Eastern Europe, and naturally supported the World Refugee Year.

She promised she would do her best to be available to launch our expedition in person. That was all I could ask for. I folded up the maps while waiting to be shown out. There was an extra spring in my step on the way to my hotel.

About a month before our start, Princess Grace sent a note saying that sadly, she would have to decline our invitation because of a family engagement. We were deeply disappointed, but I was enriched by having met such an exceptionally beautiful person.

JUMBO'S JOURNEY BEGINS

July 20, 1959: Good morning, Hannibal. This is the first day of our journey and quest to rediscover your route over the Alps. We seem to have enough information— particularly from Polybius—to know your passage. We have been able to procure a young elephant for the journey and hope to learn something of your difficulties and triumphs in our reenactment of your crossing. We believe we are the first to take an elephant along your route since you did, so, in a sense, we will be traveling with you.

I have so many questions. How did you feed the elephants? We're guessing that you did not make them carry anything except platforms on their backs to conserve their strength. What was it like for you personally to command a large army? How strict were you with high standards for your officers and men? How

TURIN (finish) ← plains of the Po river

SUSA

frontier ridge between France and Italy.

Col de Mt Cenis →

← Col de Clapier

le Planey

L'Esseillon

E

S

N

W

la Praz

Route of the British Alpine Hannibal Expedition (looking south-east)

St Michel

La Chambre

Isère

Aiguebelle

Arc

La Rochette

JMH

Start: Montmelian

River Isere

Our path across the Alps.

did you manage mercenaries? I would love to know more about your sense of humor.

We place the start of your first ascent in the mountains at Pontcharra, where you were ambushed at the gorge above the enemy town of La Rochette.

Such were the thoughts running through my mind as we set out. For weeks, I had wondered how it would be to walk with an elephant in the Alps. Now we were retracing Hannibal's route and letting our imaginations run wild as we imagined his thirty-seven elephants, their smell, their trumpeting, and the calls of their mahouts. Jumbo was striding along and clearly enjoying the hike. The long train ride from Turin to our starting point had given her none of the regular exercise she was accustomed to. Now she was ready to be moving.

The day began to heat up. The sun beat down on the dusty road, and the drone of flies hung heavily on the air as we plodded along. We became aware of how little sleep we had had the night before and began to feel the discomfort of the grueling sun.

There had been plenty of glamour, the excitement of preparations and the flurry of media coverage at the launch of our bold endeavor—but now remained the down-to-earth fact that we were actually walking with an elephant nearly a hundred fifty miles over the French and Italian Alps. I was conscious of the pressures, the surrounding crush of reporters and photographers, the varied needs of our nine-member team, the necessity for good lines of communication, the lack of an expedition car, and, by no means least, the demands of Jumbo, our two-and-a-half-ton traveling companion.

I realized it would be possible to cope with these pressures only as long as I could stay fresh mentally, physically, and spiritually, and maintain an at-least-one-move-ahead position on our day-to-day plan. At age twenty-six, I was feeling young, inexperienced, and more than a little naive, only three years out of university and with no leadership experience.

The daily plan itself was simple: When Hannibal marched, we would march. When he rested, we would rest. When he fought the Alpine tribes, we would rest!

This always brought a laugh when I lectured in later years. Then I would tell of the many unique problems our expedition faced. No Alpine warrior tribes but extensive worldwide publicity.

Our secondary task, one of the many dimensions we added as the trip evolved, was to study our elephant's behavior and speeds at varying altitudes and conditions. To do this, we used an altimeter and pedometer to obtain readings every half-hour that were entered in the expedition logbook.

At Pontcharra, we commenced the real journey "in Hannibal's tracks." Till then, it had been a matter of getting into position. Now we brought out our measuring instruments and made a careful record of Jumbo's progress.

Two members of the team—Richard and Colonel Hickman, our veterinary officer—went ahead to have a close look at the steepest section of the climb to the Col de Clapier, our destination nine days on, while the rest of the team, together with Jumbo, three mules, and their drivers, passed on through Pontcharra toward the "ascent."

The gorge narrowed until it was barely wide enough for the road and a single-track railway. It seemed likely that in such surroundings, Hannibal had fought his first challenging battle. La Rochette, twelve miles from Pontcharra, had been a strategically positioned town in 218 B.C., no meager site to capture.

Jumbo's speed was steady, and she was obviously enjoying the whole thing except for the flies. The pedometer was not quite as accurate as we had hoped, but its readings were consistent.

If Hannibal had taken La Rochette by surprise, as we believed, while many of its inhabitants were out fighting his men in the gorge, we certainly did not arrive unnoticed. One enthusiastic onlooker assured me that the town had never seen so many people. I added "since Hannibal's forty thousand." We laughed. At La Rochette, Jumbo's fans had waited hours to see her. The market was packed with people. Children were everywhere. A kind of Western cowboy corral surrounded the square. In the center stood two long tables covered with dazzling white linen and generous supplies of local wine. Everyone was talking excitedly, so pleased that we had come, so pleased to see *l'elephant*. What could be finer than a large, lovable animal to add to the celebration?

The town band played with great gusto. It was much smaller and more personal than the prior day's at Montmélian, with the musicians wearing a mixture of uniforms and everyday work clothes.

After the national anthems of France and Britain and the *vin d'honneur*, a rotund man led forward a tiny donkey named Albert that was pulling a bright yellow cart piled high with vegetables and fruit. Albert and Jumbo didn't seem to like each other, but Jumbo ate her fill. After this initial greeting, we were invited to a grand reception and dinner hosted by the mayor.

We walked wearily but contentedly to the campsite that had been prepared carefully by team members Michael and Baldi, our truck driver. The setting was ideal, an open field beside a barn with running water near at hand. Ernesto tethered Jumbo to a sufficiently stout tree, and fed her a good meal while the rest of us pitched tents and got ready for the mayor's reception.

My first leadership decision was to have our team leave the lavish banquet early. It may have been considered rude to our hosts and was a drastic measure by a leader who did not often ignore the yearnings of his stomach. But I knew it was better to do this than get to bed at 1 a.m., as on the previous night. I chalked this up as the first time I had to exercise firm authority over the team. Rich desserts were about to crown the feast, but I knew that we needed the rest.

The banquet demonstrated one of our biggest problems: getting overtired and overfed. Additionally, there was the likelihood of being discourteous to the many generous hosts we would meet along the way. I scribbled closing notes to the day's log readings by flashlight and then, aching and exhausted, climbed into my sleeping bag under a full moon. Only fifteen yards away loomed Jumbo. The moonlight shone through dancing leaves stirred by the evening breeze, and played exotic patterns on her broad, bristled back. This journey seemed like a fantastic dream. I was content. We had marched through the first day's itinerary, and all was well.

> *Hannibal, at this stage, you would have already lost a lot of men, but you managed to capture a prosperous town. This was your toughest fighting since leaving Spain. But you have won provisions for the hard days ahead. Your elephants are safe and well fed.*

WILD ELEPHANT

Polybius was our master guide, so we referred to him each day. On the fifth day of the journey, as we arrived in Saint-Michel, we read:

> *The natives came out to meet Hannibal . . . holding olive branches and wreaths. He was suspicious of such proffers of alliance and took great pains to find out what their motives were. They told him that they knew about the capture of [La Rochette] and the destruction of those who had attempted to do him wrong. They assured him they neither wished to inflict nor to suffer any injuries. They promised to give him hostages. He finally agreed to their proposals and feigned acceptance of their friendship. Upon delivery of hostages and provision of cattle, Hannibal trusted them so far as to employ them as guides.*

Taking this meeting into full account and to fit our itinerary as exactly as possible with Hannibal's, we did not leave Saint-Michel until the afternoon of the fifth day. It seemed reasonable to assume that when the Carthaginians stopped at this point, half a day was spent in assessing the situation and negotiating terms. For us, setting aside the morning to cover such delays and, incidentally, for the expedition to have much-needed rest, was not only expedient but also followed Hannibal's timetable. We spent the morning catching up on sleep, working on neglected portions of the logbook, shopping, reorganizing our equipment, and reading newspapers.

It was important for us to keep tuned in to the outside world, though at times it seemed an abstraction compared with the immediacy of the journey. We had been brought into French politics and found that *L'Express* had cottoned onto the "elephant story" in a big way. It was using it as a source for satirical cartoons headed *"Vive l'elephrance,"* which portrayed a variety of curious animals, including the gaullephant, with the head of General de Gaulle.

We wanted to work with the press as closely and amiably as possible. Of course, Stephen Barber and John Silverside of the *News-Chronicle* as well as Tim Green and David Lees of *Life* magazine received special treatment, as their publications had underwritten our expedition. The *Chronicle* had published an impressive buildup to the climb, with a section of the front page dedicated to our daily progress. A full week before the start, there was a large picture of one of Jumbo's boots on the cover with the bold, eye-catching caption: "Can you guess what this queer object is?" The newspaper went on to announce that the *News-Chronicle* had secured exclusive rights to one of the most unusual and intriguing stories of the year. Three days later, there was a full page dedicated to our journey with a detailed map so that readers could follow us closely. Barber was to wire back daily comments, whimsy, and facts, such as how much weight Jumbo had lost and how fast and far she had walked.

One political cartoon went over in a big way in Britain. Harold MacMillan and his Conservative party were running for reelection. The cartoon showed "Mac Hannibal," an elephant with MacMillan's distinguishing moustache, cresting a peak called, "The Prospect of Victory," while behind were a row of his administration's problems: unemployment, inflation, Cyprus, and colonial policy. The cartoon showed the two leaders of the opposition party, Labor, muttering, "What baffles me is—how on earth did he get that far?" As I read these press cuttings, I find myself returned to the England of the 1950s.

My favorite cartoon was in *Punch*, the English humor magazine. A vast yet frisky young elephant is depicted dashing out of the London Zoo, much to the consternation of the crowds. Two zookeepers are trying unsuccessfully to catch him. One is saying: "This is the third little perisher this week that's decided to follow

Centerfold of the Life magazine issue that devoted seven pages to our expedition.

the Hannibal expedition!"That's British humor: "Little perisher" for a two-ton elephant!

We had a great relationship with the press, though tensions increased the higher we climbed. In simple terms, we wanted Jumbo as far away from any cliffs as possible; the press wanted to photograph her dangerously close to the edge.

Ancient Saint-Michel is nearly two hundred feet farther up the side of the steeply sloping north face of the Arc River than the present town. Until Napoleon's day, a huge lake was in the area. Not until he had broken the enormous natural dam there was the site of the new Saint-Michel revealed. We struggled up to the level of the old town, where Hannibal would have had to circumnavigate the lake. Our caravan took a narrow footpath to the tiny village of Orelle, where we paused for a photo shoot. Jumbo stood majestically with the dramatic mountain landscape as backdrop and proudly waved her trunk. She had a twinkle in her eye as she accepted her reward of a pear from Ernesto.

At this point, the path divided, and we were unsure of the best way to go. One route led steeply downward to the valley bottom, and the other up toward a tiny village. Our map was not very helpful, but local guides had plenty of opinions. All except one

"This is the third little perisher this week that's decided to join the Hannibal Expedition."

farmer, plump and unshaven, insisted it would be impossible to take the high road and that the only way to go was downhill. He remained insistent. He waggled the huge scythe drooping over his shoulder and looked indignantly at the others. The two *gendarmes* on bicycles who were our constant companions had recently returned from North Africa and did not know the district well. Still uncertain, inspired by a spirit of adventure, we clung to the idea that the farmer might be right.

As Jumbo drank red wine and played a borrowed harmonica—holding it in her trunk, puffing rhythmically, and lifting two feet at a time as if dancing a stately sarabande—I jumped onto the back of a Vespa scooter belonging to one of the newsmen who had followed us. We set out on a rapid reconnaissance patrol. Ten minutes later, I gave the order to take the high road: We would avoid the car traffic and crowds; the way seemed to match Hannibal's route more closely; the condition of the trail appeared ideal, easy for Jumbo's feet with no jagged rocks; and the views were magnificent.

Our new guide, his scythe over shoulder, led the way enthusiastically. The road narrowed. Car drivers gave up following us, and we passed through another, smaller village. The look of utter astonishment on the villagers' faces was delightful. I am sure that news of Jumbo's travels had not reached this remote outpost.

The road leveled out, and Jimmy went ahead to see if the bridge over a torrent would hold Jumbo. His technique consisted of inspecting each bridge structure, sometimes climbing under it to examine its foundation. Jumbo seemed naturally conscious of her vast weight and would not easily commit herself to apparently fragile structures. No one else was allowed on a bridge at the same time, since if Jumbo were to sidestep or try to turn around, they risked being crushed against a railing or even pushed into the current below. Now, seeing that all was clear, Jimmy beckoned the caravan forward. Ernesto gently led Jumbo across while her trunk felt the way ahead to make sure it was safe. Bridge crossings became routine, but of course, everything depended on the condition of the bridges.

The higher the bridge, the more cautious we became. When Ernesto led Jumbo over, everyone stood back and waited until she was safely across. Then we would follow. Otherwise, we tended to gather around Jumbo as we climbed rather than be strung along the trail. She was our focal point.

Every mahout has an *ankus*, a hand tool with a curved spike on one end, for guiding his elephant. Ernesto's had a very small spike that was effective in prodding Jumbo to get going or to change direction.

Eventually, the path grew extremely narrow and started to run downhill very steeply, one foot down for every four feet forward. Below we could see the press cars waiting. Even the Vespa rider had had to turn back. We made slow progress, but Jumbo's trunk was invaluable in such steep situations, helping her find good footholds with confidence.

As our guide had said, the high road turned out to be by far the more interesting route and, certainly more like Hannibal's than the main motor road. But it took us longer than estimated to reach our campsite for the night. As we descended, my mind was on the situation there, though I knew the advance team would have the tents up. There were dark clouds overhead and a mean wind that suddenly blew cold, causing us concern. It was no good trying to hurry. Jumbo had to take her time down the steep descent; this called for patience.

La Praz was in a lonely spot by a brook. As anticipated, Michael and Colonel Hickman had pitched camp, set up the tents, cordoned them off, and were peeling potatoes and slicing beans. We had roped off our tents to keep away excited local youths who continually rushed through the camp making wild noises. One of them pretended not to hear the colonel's warning, but his French might have been incomprehensible. As the colonel tried addressing the boy in German, an old woman came up, convinced that this was a German expedition, and vehemently expressed her dislike of Germany. The colonel was able finally to quiet her.

As soon as Jumbo arrived, she became the center of attraction. The rope cordon was transferred from the campsite to her. This took some time as it had to be out of the elephant's reach with her six-foot trunk from where she was chained to tree.

Suddenly it grew dark and bitterly cold, and rain started pouring down. The "reception committee," including the press, scattered into the night in an effort to keep dry. High on a mountainside, we were left to face an ugly monster of a storm. It felt like the worst storm I could imagine, and I suddenly had apprehension that something terrible was going to happen. It was as if all the forces of nature were being hurled at unprepared us. Darkness had come early because of the heavy, low-lying clouds. Before we had had a chance to settle down, the storm broke. Rain came in torrents, sleeting in through the tent openings as the wind shifted. Why was it that on the one night we had arrived near to sunset, all the elements seemed to conspire against us (including the fact that we were also low on food). I thought I would be able to get my fears under control, but with them came the insidious suggestion that the expedition was vulnerable. Fortunately, I realized again that our team members were characterized by maturity and stamina.

Along with the deep rumble and crackle of thunder and flashes of lightning, the Primus stove sputtered and died. Baldi had the presence of mind to pull a tarpaulin over the bales of hay and the cardboard boxes of supplies on the truck. We found that a Tilley lamp we had depended on for heat as well as for light had broken, and the other one fizzled and took a long time to relight. The ground was soaked, and the nearby stream was turning our field into a swamp.

Clare had been sitting over a pot of soup coming to a boil on the Primus when the wild moment of wet darkness hit. She valiantly nursed it throughout the gloom and cold while everyone else rushed around. When we were feeling most miserable, we knew that Clare's hot soup would warm and encourage us.

Ernesto's concern, of course, was for Jumbo, who was tired, hungry, wet, and unable to see in the pitch darkness. In the hubbub of arrival, he had somehow mislaid his ankus. We could hear the huge, two-ton thunderbolt tearing at her chain and thrashing around in the undergrowth. In addition to everything else, we had to contend with an elephant who was nearly out of control. Then there came the wildest call I have ever heard, the trumpeting squeal of a crazed elephant. It rose above the wind, carried urgently up the valley and echoing back. If that midnight fury had broken loose from her moorings and borne down upon the camp, there would have been very little left of either us or our equipment. However, Ernesto provided the crucial response to the danger. He managed to find his ankus and spoke very gently but firmly to Jumbo, quieting her down. The closeness of those two, mahout and elephant, saved the day.

Coming close and cupping his hand to my ear, Ernesto yelled that Jumbo needed a shelter. I yelled back, "I'm off to find one!" Then to Cynthia, who was propping up a fallen tent, I called, "Come on! Let's find a home for Jumbo."

With torches beaming through sheets of rain, Cynthia and I, bent double in the squall, pushed our way through the lank grass, leaving Ernesto to deal with Jumbo and the others to get our equipment into tents. Down in the valley, we could see a tiny light, so we angled toward it without any sense of a path. We stumbled to the door of a farmhouse, grateful that a light had been left on outside. Otherwise we would never have found the place.

The family was sitting in the kitchen, warm and cozy. I remember the smoke as it drifted up from an open fireplace to the ceiling. Every detail remains in my memory—a shaggy sheepdog getting up and coming to us with wagging tail. It was a simple scene but to us—wet and shivering strangers—it looked unspeakably warm and inviting. In our broken French, we pleaded with the family for shelter for our elephant. The farmer instantly donned his waterproof coat and led me to his barn. It was filled with bleating goats and stacked with hay, but there might be room for an elephant. Cynthia stayed chatting with the family until, after what seemed hours to her, the farmer and I came back.

Cynthia went back to the barn with us, where we shooed the goats to another enclosure and thanked the generous farmer. I still remember the smells of that barn: damp hay, animal waste, rotting garbage. Yet the barn signaled shelter for Jumbo! With this happy news, we climbed up the hill to our beleaguered campsite. Even though the rain now blew right into our faces, the knowledge of a safe haven for Jumbo cheered us. We had been gone about twenty minutes. The narrow beam of my torch fell on the area around Jumbo's tree. It was a scene of complete chaos. Small trees that had been within her reach now lay broken and splintered on the ground. The rope we had so carefully placed out of reach of her trunk, she had caught and twisted around herself. It needed Ernesto's full patience and strength of mind to unravel that knot and quiet her down. By this time, though, she had been fed. We were able to move her to the barn without delay. I could not praise Ernesto enough for the way he handled the situation; he was magnificent in calming Jumbo. Elephants and humans have similar lifespans and can develop an amazing symbiosis. I am convinced that Ernesto and Jumbo had developed this to a remarkable degree. That night had certainly put their relationship to the test.

The rain continued to pour down. Our group huddled over cups of hot soup in the driest of the tents. We felt we were experiencing some of the conditions the Carthaginians had faced. But they had snow as well! The kind farmer and his family allowed several team members to sleep in the barn. The rest of us stayed in the driest tent and left the other tents as empty, flapping monuments to the weather. I was out like a light as soon as my head touched the pillow. A deep sense of peace had come over me, knowing that Jumbo was safe and no one was hurt.

It is now more than fifty years later, and I am thinking back to that dreadful night. With the variability of alpine weather, it might seem almost inevitable that we should have faced such conditions along the way. In this case, the conditions were extreme and the timing was terrible. How prepared should we have been? There had always been a major risk factor as we planned for the expedition. We had weighed the risks and felt confident to go ahead. Now we had faced a crucial test, which we passed but only barely and with an enormous amount of gratitude to everyone involved, including Jumbo. The lesson taught me that when weighing risks, having the right team and the right attitude must be factored in. Certainly in our case, attitude, morale, and a reliable team meant that we were able to pull through at crucial moments, after seeing what had seemed to be wise decisions go awry.

Little things can make a huge difference. If the farmer had not left his front door light on, we would never have found his barn, the safe shelter for Jumbo. I am grateful that our torches worked, that nobody got hurt, and for the courage and determination shown by everyone on the team, especially Ernesto. The next day, despite lack of sleep, everyone—including Jumbo—woke cheerful, refreshed, and ready to go.

I also consider the fear. How did fear affect each one of us, including Jumbo? How does it weigh on the spirit? How does it affect judgment? I know that I was learning wisdom through fear: healthy fear, not the paralyzing kind. I certainly experienced it that night, and the dread of what might have happened if Jumbo had broken loose and gone wild remains a vivid memory.

In the planning stages of the expedition, I had been presented by a keeper at the Whipsnade Zoo with a strong case for taking two elephants, as companionship means so much to them. But finances and practicality made it impossible. I am reminded of the quote by Scott Cairns: May your afflictions be few but may you not squander them. If the dark night of the storm was an "affliction," I was determined to be the wiser for it. I believe strongly in God's providence. In one sense our experience that night was to teach us a lesson on the limits of risk, making us more cautious for our ultimate good and the success of our enterprise.

THE NIGHT CLIMB

> *Next day the enemy made their departure. Hannibal joined his cavalry, pack horses, and elephants and advanced to the summit of the pass. He no longer encountered any large force of the enemy but was molested by a few. . . for some had taken advantage of the ground and attacked him from two sides.*
>
> —Polybius

The idea of a secret night climb had come to us earlier while discussing Polybius with Dr. McDonald. It explained why Hannibal had to "join" (in fact, rejoin) his cavalry, pack horses, and elephants in this way, to escape attacks from barbarian tribes. The implication was that they must have had an earlier start.

It was one thing to dream up the idea in the comfort of a professor's elegant rooms at Cambridge University and another to stir one's weary bones and rise at two o'clock in the morning and get moving. However, we were making history and about to do something not attempted since Hannibal's day. We dressed in our warmest clothing and groped our way around the camp, locating equipment and packing.

A late moon was rising above the mountains, and the great rock faces of L'Esseillon shone in the eerie light. There was not a rustle from the trees that crowned the natural fortress. Only the distant rush of water over the steep slopes disturbed the silence. Richard and the colonel checked the equipment we wanted to have handy: compass, altimeter, pedometer, thermometer, flash-lights, Tilley lamp, large-scale map, flambeau torches, and matches to light them. For sustenance, we had sandwiches and fruit, chocolate, glucose tablets, and water. A special treat of a bucket of carrots was awaiting Jumbo at Le Planey.

We were now ready to leave. Michael and Baldi were left be-hind to pack up the tents, load all our equipment into the truck, and follow at their leisure. Jumbo's boots were left in the truck. If she needed them—though she never did—they would not be far away. Ernesto's voice carried clearly from the shadows as he spoke in soft undertones. "Forward, Jumbo. Forward, Jumbo. Leg lift, lift, Jumbo, lift."

He undid the chain holding her to a suitably stout tree and threw it over her shoulder with a clatter, fastening it firmly around her neck. That chain could well be considered one of our most important pieces of equipment. It had to be strong, as Jumbo would pull at her moorings during the night with enor-mous force. Once "adrift," she would be off who knows where. The only one strong enough to carry the heavy chain was Jumbo herself, who seemed to ignore its great weight. With a command from Ernesto, her huge bulk lurched out of the shadows into bright moonlight. I gave the word to start our trek.

Then the press—the ones who knew what was going on—ar-rived. Tim Green and Pierre Boulat of *Life* and John Silverside and Stephen Barber of the *News-Chronicle*, with his wife, showed up in time to see us break camp. Then they went on down the steep, winding path to the gorge to prepare for photographs.

The friendly rivalry between different sections of the press was amusing. Before Tim and Pierre set out from the hotel at 1 a.m., they left a note for the *Paris-Match* team: *Hope you had a good night! You will not find Jumbo at L'Esseillon if you fancy going to go there.*

We were off, down the tortuous path that wound toward the valley floor below. The caravan slowly moved forward, Jumbo setting the pace and everyone eager to see how she would react to this unusual experience. Quite suddenly, we came to a narrow gorge where huge rock slabs rose on either side of the path. At one time, this was the only way up to the fort at L'Esseillon after the rock had been laboriously blasted away to widen it enough for cannon and vehicle. Here, the press were waiting with flash-lamps at the ready and a merry word of welcome. Our flaming torches cast long shadows behind us and onto Jumbo's vast flanks, making the scene into as close a replica of the Carthaginian descent as could be imagined.

The path down from the fort was uneven, with loose stones and sand, but it was easy enough to see our way. The rain clouds had vanished, and we could see stars, including the constellations of Orion and the Pleiades, while the moon, now almost full, shone on our path with clear, soft light. Our flaming torches were nearly out by the time the caravan reached the Arc River. After crossing it, there was a stretch of main motor road to cover before arriving at Bramans, the next village, but at three in the morning, the traffic was extremely light. One or two cars came past, driving too fast to notice the unusual sight, but one motorist clearly had the fright of his life. Jumbo and party were keeping to the right of the road as the noisy machine approached from the other direction. As the car drew near, he raised his head suddenly with wide-eyed amazement. The vehicle swerved away from us, nearly hit the curb, and then shot off as fast as it could into the darkness.

Bramans lay still in the moonlight as we passed down its narrow, dark main street. A pause at the village fountain for Jumbo's sake led to some good flash photographs and rather louder talking among the ranks than was necessary.

One newspaper reported that Jumbo was so quiet she could pass through villages without waking anyone. Next morning, though, one old lady complained bitterly to Jimmy that the noise had woken her. We apologized profusely, but it was of little avail as the root of the matter was disappointment. She had expected to enjoy the sight of Jumbo's approach in afternoon sun, not as a phantom in the moonlight.

From the village, the road wound up steeply through innumerable twists and turns. Jumbo was climbing magnificently. In spite of the forty-degree temperature—cold for her—and the difficult conditions, never a murmur, never an audible comment; she just walked on steadily and as softly as if on tiptoe. After a long climb of about one foot elevation in seven, during which Jumbo showed no slackening of pace, we stopped for rest and a makeshift "breakfast." We were exhausted. Our adrenalin had drained away. The colonel wisely produced a flask of brandy, and it cheered us all up.

Clare had stayed behind, writing in the logbook. To catch up, she took a shortcut over the top of a rocky peninsula that we were circumnavigating. As she slid down the steep bank toward us, she dislodged a stone. As soon as Jumbo heard the sound, she wheeled sharply toward it with such speed that anyone in the way would have been knocked flat. Elephants have sensitive hearing, but none of us knew that they, and Jumbo in particular, were apprehensive about falling rocks.

The road was leveling now, and we knew that most of the climbing was over for the time being. An extremely steep drop on one side of the path had to be watched carefully. As dawn broke through the mist and started to drench the beautiful, high Alpine valley with golden sunshine, the expedition arrived at Le Planey. By this time, our fatigue had worn off. After a couple of hours' rest, we were all for carrying straight on up La Crosta toward the Col de Clapier. But that was unrealistic. There was the press to consider.

It was Sunday, and Silverside would not be able to send his photographs of this crucial section back to the *News-Chronicle* since the transmission line was out of action on weekends. Moreover, as far as the world was concerned, the expedition was still at L'Esseillon. Being two steps ahead could lead to a great deal of confusion and chaos. We decided to wait and conform to our initial plan of undertaking the ascent of La Crosta to the Col de Clapier on Monday.

By coming so far up the valley during the night march, we clearly demonstrated that Hannibal's elephants could easily have reached the Col de Clapier in a night and a day. Hannibal was attacked intermittently, and probably had a more difficult path over the stretch to Le Planey. But we could estimate an allowance for this and still found the distance well within his reach. It had not been until we actually did the march to Le Planey by night that we were convinced it was possible.

When in 1936, Richard Halliburton took an elephant over the Great St. Bernard Pass, he wrote that his charge was affected by the altitude. If Jumbo had been similarly afflicted, she would never have made the Le Planey climb. Until now, the only information on the effect of high altitude on elephants was Halliburton's experiment. But we were now demonstrating that an elephant could manage higher altitudes, over six thousand feet above sea level.

Jumbo was hungry, and the expedition's food supply had not yet come up the valley. While we were asking a farmer if he could spare some hay, Jumbo inquisitively poked her trunk through the open window of a roadside cabin. Two girls came to the window smiling, and we laughed together. It must have been a little frightening, however, to see a twisting proboscis feeling its way in through the window. Nevertheless, the discovery that it was Jumbo would no doubt be ample compensation.

At Le Planey, we were welcomed to the magnificent chalet of Dr. M.A. de Lavis-Trafford, who had been described by journalists as "the British Hannibal authority." The first time we met him had been at the Carlton Club in London, where Richard and I were invited for a discussion over lunch. The doctor was in his eighties, full of life and in fine form talking about Hannibal. A man of letters and of considerable fortune, he had an imposing presence and a booming voice.

He generously let us camp on his property by the river in Le Planey. It was the perfect spot with a spacious lawn and a good strong tree for Jumbo. As soon as the tents were erected and sleeping bags unrolled, team members crept in and slept. Meanwhile, the rest of the press corps had started to arrive to catch up on the news. Though the idea of a night march had taken them by surprise, they took it well, laughed uproariously, and saw the method of our madness in emulating Hannibal's forced march.

Three of us went back down the valley in the expedition car to contact the disappointed community of Bramans. Specifically, we had to make peace with the mayor, who was understandably irate. By stealing through his village at night, we had disrupted his plans for a reception for Jumbo. I apologized profusely. We agreed that the problem was a breakdown in communication, and he understood when I mentioned that we had passed through villages larger than Bramans without any reception.

It all ended happily after we invited the mayor and all who could join him from the village to come for a *vin d'honneur* at Le Planey, offering our lorry to bring the children for the party. Three

Trying on Jumbo's new boots and jacket.

of us raced to Modane to buy the best wine and returned to the camp by lunchtime. When we didn't have wine glasses for sixty people, our host came to the rescue. From the depths of his chalet, out they came—brand-new wine glasses packed in straw. Together with the rather Bohemian assortment of mugs belonging to expedition members, we had just enough vessels to drink from. Jumbo stood quietly resting while trestle tables were brought out from the chalet and placed in front of her, and, in due course, wine and hors d'oeuvres were passed around. Having been feted and invited to an endless succession of *vins d'honneur* during the last few days, we now reversed the process and were feting the friendly villagers of Bramans as an apology for having disrupted their plans. We had been caught up in the complexities of twentieth-century public relations, festivity, and lack of communications.

As a diversion, Baldi made himself the center of attraction by serving as barber for an old farmer who had been standing near his front door with a mirror trying to trim the wisps and ends of his straggly gray hair. Baldi noticed, got a chair, and brought the man near where Jumbo was standing. He stood behind his new client, snipping and roaring with laughter as the gray hairs fell. The farmer was pleased with his haircut.

With one issue happily settled to the sounds of tinkling glasses and laughter, something more serious took its place. Throughout the afternoon, newsmen and members of the expedition had been exploring La Crosta, the only tricky part of the way ahead to our ultimate destination, the Col de Clapier itself. La Crosta ("The Crust") is the steep, rocky slope connecting the Ambin valley, in which Le Planey lies, to the six-mile plateau leading to Clapier. The path is narrow and quite steep in places. After meandering gently through woodland, it strikes uphill and eventually zigzags steeply to the Clapier plateau.

To this landscape was added an entirely unforeseen psychological and relational element that now became clear. The buildup of the previous week's journey had been enormous, as was the world interest. Jumbo was no longer just an elephant; she was a celebrated personality. We began to question the safety of taking Jumbo up La Crosta and then on to the exposed reaches of the Col de Clapier. After supper, the entire team set out for a final look at the difficult path ahead. There were three factors to consider. The most important was the safety and well-being of Jumbo. The next was the weather; a storm was forecast for the next two days. And the final factor was our relationship with the outside world. As we stood on the steep, winding path with the last rays of the setting sun illuminating the treetops, we were uncertain about risking bringing Jumbo triumphantly up to the Col de Clapier.

The elephant could have managed it—if there were no disturbances. But we could not get out of our minds her agitation at the falling rock that Clare had dislodged earlier. The photographs the press would take the next day might well be by far the most exciting of the whole trip, so we could anticipate a large number of news photographers and reporters. If anyone climbed onto the rocks overlooking the narrow stretches and dislodged stones, Jumbo might suddenly turn and cause an accident, either knocking someone off the path or slipping off herself. In theory, we could control the spectators and members of the press. In practice, many photographers would be willing to risk their own necks and might disregard the safety of others in their efforts to get spectacular photographs. We were no longer in complete control of the situation.

Sometimes complexity overwhelms planned choices. Night had fallen, and our hesitant procession climbed back down to the camp. As we sat around the campfire with bowls of soup, each team member expressed his or her view. When all had been said, I knew that I would make the final decision. I paid particular attention to the comments from Ernesto and the colonel. If we had learned anything from our experiences, it was that Jumbo was a full-fledged member of the expedition. We had come to know her as a friend, an untiring road companion, and an intelligent being who had shared our experiences. She was enjoying the trip as much as we were. If she could only add her voice to ours as to the feasibility of attempting La Crosta, the problem would have been a good deal simpler. But there she stood, silent in the darkness, quietly swinging her trunk and munching her supper. It was her climb tomorrow that mattered—not ours. If a climber takes a calculated risk on a mountain and is injured, it is the climber's own fault. With Jumbo, it was different. Our decision might lead her to be injured.

Finally, we had to face the fact that if the predicted storm hit in the next day or two, Jumbo would face it with little protection. The two broken-down shelters near the pass had no roofs. The jacket Jumbo wore on many of the cold mountain nights, although waterproof and well-insulated, had not been adequate protection from the previous high-altitude storm. We had survived at La Praz but now were well aware of the dangers. We had contracted with Signor Terni to care for Jumbo. Now we had an unwritten contract with Jumbo herself. It added new meaning to our responsibilities.

There was silence. I turned to the others. "No, we won't go up La Crosta tomorrow," I said. "We will have to find another route." To my relief, the team agreed unanimously. We were all prepared to not only stand by the decision but also to defend it against criticisms that could be leveled at us during the coming days. The tension was broken, and we tidied the campsite, walked over to Jumbo to say our customary "Good night," and climbed into our sleeping bags. My mind was buzzing with rationalizations and circuitous thoughts.

If we had been at war or in anything like the situation facing Hannibal, there would have been no question. Jumbo would have gone up "and she would have succeeded," I muttered aloud, under my breath with a tone of frustration. Ours was purely a journey of historical investigation. It was not vital that we climb to the pass. While it was a very real aim, we had never called it our most important goal. That, rather, was to test our elephant on the day-to-day basis of Hannibal's march and to study the effect of the altitude.

The entire world was now focused on our expedition. People everywhere knew that this was "the big climb." Animal lovers worldwide were getting to know Jumbo as a personality. The newspapers had not been slow to paint as human a picture as possible of our dear, lumbering companion. The daily reports in the *News-Chronicle* were appealing: Jumbo had lost such-and-such weight (which was good for her), eaten many delicious dinners, danced and played her harmonica for eager audiences, and become a hero to the British public. But on the other hand, the Societies for the Prevention of Cruelty to Animals were poised to criticize us if there was a hint of inflicting pain on Jumbo. We maintained excellent relations with them but knew that they could be critical of the whole enterprise.

Balanced against all this were many other factors. The public and press would be disappointed. The sheer sense of achievement and satisfaction of conquering La Crosta would have been profound. Was pride creeping into the picture? It would be a fine tribute to Jumbo, and to Signor Terni, who had done so much to make our journey possible. Even though I had made the decision to find another way and had the full backing of my team, I was torn between the two choices.

It was hard to get to sleep. I prayed to the Lord to give my mind peace. I sensed His presence. The next day would be one of great challenge, psychologically and physically, and I needed all the strength I could muster.

At five-thirty the next morning, Colonel Hickman, Richard, and I were preparing for a press conference. Had we been about to attempt La Crosta, there would have been an early start anyway, so we had scheduled a press conference for six to inform the press of our plans for the ascent. The colonel would have given detailed instructions as to where and when the press could go for the climb itself. However, all this was unnecessary because of my decision of the previous evening. It had been made so late that it was impossible to pass word down the valley to the newsmen that they could all sleep in.

Dr. de Lavis-Trafford had offered the use of his chalet for our press conference. At ten minutes to six, he had lighted a beautiful old brass oil-lamp and was placing chairs in an orderly fashion around a great oak table. The lighting, the dark mellow furniture and low-beamed ceiling gave the occasion a warm, intimate atmosphere. There were several newsmen, most of them from major papers. We sat down, followed by a moment's silence as I reviewed the statement spread out before me. It seemed unreal, especially so early in the morning. I shook myself. Had we really decided not to ascend La Crosta? There it was in writing.

The news would be difficult to break; I had a lump in my throat as I spoke quietly. The newsmen sat forward in their chairs in keen anticipation. The soft lamplight played on all in benevolent impartiality. My emotions were mixed. On one hand, the disappointment of not taking Jumbo up La Crosta to the Col de Clapier weighed heavily on my sense of achievement and courage. On the other, it was a relief to know that the new way ahead would be safer, whatever it would be. I briefly explained the problem we faced, the new element in the situation, and our late-night decision to bypass La Crosta. Though Jumbo's safety had been a key consideration, I explained that our decision in no way weakened the argument that Hannibal used the Col de Clapier, since this pass satisfied Polybius's description very well. The challenge for the day would be to find a better and safer way over.

Colonel Hickman took up the train of our reasoning and spoke in detail of the hazards of the ascent. After a brief period of answering questions, we collected our papers and rose to leave. Excited conversations began; everyone was as disappointed as we were. The fact remained that these same representatives of the world's press would be the first to criticize the expedition if any accident occurred on La Crosta. The more danger and excitement on that stretch, the more dramatic would be their reports. This was not a principle we could entertain. Outside were more newsmen and eager villagers, clustering around, eager for the latest news.

A mountaineer in lederhosen pushed his way through the crowd. He was tanned, rugged, and had a bristling beard. He said he knew of another way that would not cause any risks or difficulty. A local gendarme vehemently disagreed with him, arguing that the way would be too steep. We brought out maps, and the mountaineer pointed out the way. Halfway back to Bramans, a steep valley ran northward up the fierce rock buttresses of Mont Bellecombe. Beyond this was a path that crossed the high ridge, linking Bellecombe and Mont Froid at nearly nine thousand feet. It then descended to the entrance of the great valley that terminated at the Col de Clapier.

It was a moment for quick decision. Our team drew aside to discuss the information. If we were delayed an extra day to find a new and better route without having to take the main motor road up to the Col de Mont Cenis, it would be worth exploring. If there was a chance of our using this ingeniously thought-out route without having to return to the Arc River, it was worth considering.

Within minutes, we formed a reconnaissance patrol, consisting of the colonel, Ernesto and myself. Our local guides were the mountaineer and two frontier policemen. As we set off down the valley after a light breakfast, we were exhilarated. The dawn had come in its glory, and the valley was filled with a magic light. Our path looked hopeful, but it soon started to rise steeply.

As we climbed, the sheer length of the ascent began to strike us. It just went on and on at a gradient of one in four feet. The tricky passages could all be handled with a little careful forethought. But it was the ruthless, sheer, dogged climbing that eventually made us collapse onto the rocky pitch, talk the matter over for a few minutes, and decide that Jumbo should not go this way.

We returned to camp exhausted and crestfallen. The reconnaissance had been arranged in such a hurry that we were not sure what our next move should be. My inner voice said, "Slow down, slow down. If you rush things, you will be in trouble." So as compensation to the press and all those others who had managed to get up to Le Planey at such an early hour, we arranged a public trying-on of Jumbo's boots. This caused much interest and merriment for the team and the press. Jumbo seemed happy with them, for they fit well, but clearly preferred not to wear them.

After more mid-morning team discussion, we reluctantly decided to take the expedition back to the Arc River and find a route away from the main motor road to the Col de Mont Cenis. Colonel Hickman and Stephen Barber set out to explore a route suggested by the two gendarmes through the Forêt d'Arc. While Jumbo and the rest of our team returned to Bramans and the river, the colonel and Barber scouted out this new way and came back to us with great excitement. The path was manageable: It wound up the mountainside, through the woods, and then above the tree line toward the Col de Mont Cenis, our alternative pass. The way was steep, ascending over two thousand feet, but without tricky, dangerous parts as on La Crosta.

The scouts had come upon an isolated chapel refuge, and an old curé had come out to welcome them. On hearing that they were from the Hannibal expedition, he said, "Ah, yes. I have in my old records some tales that Hannibal may have even come this way." I received the news of this alternative route with delight, and immediately got out the maps to calculate its further feasibility. It was going to be a long, steady climb tomorrow but well within Jumbo's capability. We started to plan our next two days' itinerary. We had the colonel and Barber to thank for this discovery.

One thing was clear. We could now estimate when we would cross the Col de Mont Cenis and inform the mayor of Susa, our first town in Italy, when we planned to arrive. This was important as we knew he was planning a grand celebration for the whole city.

It was a joy to revisit the village of Bramans in broad daylight. I was pleased to know that the one village that had never been able to see Jumbo, because of the night march, had her now passing through on view to everyone in the street, delighting the villagers, particularly the children, who were wearing homemade Carthaginian helmets and wielding beautifully carved swords.

From there we turned northeast along the Arc River, and decided to camp near the village of Termignon. On the way we were met by a group of children from the hamlet of La Villette. Excitedly they danced around us, the younger ones garlanded with wreaths of wildflowers, bound together with cornstalks. The two oldest girls, rosy-cheeked with luxuriant black hair, smiled shyly. As the children scampered along, they sang a pretty folk song with all the words now celebrating our elephant. Each new verse added another elephant to the expedition. Their voices faded into the distance and left a sense of sweet nostalgia.

By late afternoon we reached Termignon, well upstream from Bramans. This village was at the very base of the steep ascent planned for the next morning. Our advance team under Richard had contacted the very surprised mayor and procured a good campsite outside the village. Then, because of impending stormy weather, Richard looked for shelter for Jumbo, finding a large, comfortable stable. We were grateful for it even though we couldn't camp close to Jumbo. After settling down with our tents in an even, grassy pasture, we went into the village for dinner at a little hotel. It was the first restaurant meal for the team since before our start. Michael remained at the stable to guard Jumbo, letting Ernesto relax and join us. We were in high spirits, as there had been a whole day to consider yesterday's decision. Our team had new unity, giving us extra strength. The public's warm understanding and sympathy had been encouraging. Love of Jumbo was becoming our overarching theme.

But we sensed a nagging apprehension. As expedition leader, I felt this deeply. Just as dinner was finishing, Signor Terni of the Turin Zoo arrived and joined us for a drink of rich port. He was anxious to discover why we had not ascended La Crosta and, more important, whether Jumbo was happy and in good health. The story of the decision came out over a second round of drinks. Afterward, we walked with Signor Terni to Jumbo's stable to wish her a good night. She was clearly pleased to see him. Ernesto assured us that Jumbo would be ready for the next morning's strenuous climb.

How does an elephant express pleasure? Jumbo certainly could, by a particularly endearing swing of her trunk, gentle rumbling noises down her throat, and some flapping of her ears. We parted from Signor Terni knowing that he was pleased with our decision and the fact that our primary aim had been Jumbo's safety. As we walked back to the campsite, the evening light lit up the surrounding peaks.

Back at camp I was ready to collapse into my sleeping bag. My journal entry that evening reads: *About to go to bed. Barber came in late. Long hot session about change in plans. Made peace with all at the end. Off to bed at last, so tired, at 12:30.*

What was all that about? As I write this more than fifty years later, trying to unearth the reason for this ruckus, it appears that over those last few days, Stephen Barber had wanted an increasing role in our planning and execution. Instead of being simply the appointed reporter for his paper, he was getting more deeply involved. I was so grateful that he had assisted Colonel Hickman in scouting our route up to the Col de Mont Cenis, and didn't feel consciously bothered by this aspect of his relationship to our team.

Looking back over all these years and having been the founder of a Silicon Valley corporation and its president for fifty years, I am now able to assess the many decisions I made during the expedition more objectively. The change of plans was the most difficult, but now I welcome the hard edges of such a choice and the difficult relationship with Barber, as these prepared me for my life in California.

I have found that overall, there is a mysterious and intimate space where God's grace can bring a sense of peace and self-knowledge, based on trusting His love and care. Years after the 1959 expedition, it helped me maintain a degree of integrity in spite of the pressures and expectations of piloting a small company during the birth of Silicon Valley. But at that earlier stage in my life, I was only just learning this balance. It was easy for me to forget the big picture and dwell on my inadequacies. This was my first position of significant leadership and responsibility, and their demands challenged me. Those last two days had been among the most emotional of my life, and I was ready to slip into oblivion as soon as my head touched the pillow.

JUMBO'S HISTORIC CLIMB

> *After having a journey lasting nine days, Hannibal*
> *gained the summit pass. He camped there for two days to*
> *rest the survivors of his army and wait for stragglers....*
> *As it was now almost the time of the setting of the*
> *Pleiades, snow had already settled on the summit.*
> —Polybius

I have always been fascinated by the way historians were able to establish the time of year that Hannibal crossed the Alps. The clue is Polybius's mention of the setting of the Pleiades. We can determine that in 218 B.C., they set beyond the western horizon at the end of October. Therefore, we can assume that Hannibal's crossing was in October.

In 1959, the day was to start in chaos, with the stable in disarray, and end in triumph for Jumbo and the expedition. At 5:45

a.m., Richard and I went over to Jumbo's downtown stable and found Ernesto upset. During the night, Jumbo had sat on his personal possessions, squashing his suitcase, and also had eaten a pair of his trousers and chewed on his shirts. This was a new and unexpected aspect of her. Was there a darker side to Jumbo's usual benevolent nature?

More troubling, Ernesto could not find his ankus. In a panic, I borrowed a bike to go back and search the lorry at camp for the vital tool. It was crucial to have this if we were to make the two-thousand-foot ascent to the Col de Mont Cenis with Jumbo. Baldi and I searched and found the ankus behind the driver's seat. I rushed back to camp, joyfully wielding the precious implement, and Jumbo, with Ernesto now fully in command, set off with half the team after a quick breakfast.

Jumbo did not seem to need breakfast, as she had been munching her hundred fifty pounds of hay for a good part of the night, and also had enjoyed an extra bucket of oats. Passing through Termignon's deserted streets in early morning, we saw few signs of life.

To me, Termignon has always implied terminus. And it indeed was the terminus of our week's journey up the Arc River. From there, we were to zig-zag straight up the mountainside on an old trail that was seldom used and drivable only in parts. We were pleased that it was far from the busy main motor road to Italy.

The early start made sense as we were not sure how long it would take Jumbo to climb to the pass. I was getting less and less sleep, and this was having an effect on me. I needed to be able to think clearly. As I prayed, I sensed inner strength and peace returning, but with the weight of responsibility always there, I resorted to my habit of running music through my head, especially Brahms and other favorites.

When the mayor of Susa and Mr. Bateman, the British consul from Turin, appeared, we walked along with Jumbo, talking about our arrival in Susa the next day.

To pay homage to Hannibal, we felt it appropriate that on this final day of climbing, members of the expedition should ascend both the Mont Cenis and Clapier passes simultaneously. This was a group decision we had made the day before. While Jumbo was climbing steadily through thinning pines up to above the tree line, half of our team was to climb up to the Col de Clapier, the route Hannibal took. Our plan was to stand where he had stood, to point to the clearly defined Po valley, as he had done to encourage his troops. The fact that Jumbo was unable to be there did not deter us.

Stonemasons from Modane had carved an elephant image on a great slab of rock at the Col de Clapier for the occasion. Whimsically, we decided that they should not carve an inscription but should leave that for the next team if anyone else should ever choose to bring an elephant to this spot. Thus, the image stood for Jumbo and all elephants that have accomplished extraordinary things.

Jumbo climbed magnificently. It was overcast, and there were several squalls of rain, but they did not deter her. For the photographers, this was the highlight of the journey. Beyond Jumbo, steadily climbing higher and farther from the deep forests and valleys, lay ranges of majestic peaks. The great glacier of the Vanoise, stretching across the far horizon, presided over the spectacular panorama.

Meanwhile the party that was heading toward the Col de Clapier had driven to the Col du Petit Mont Cenis. This meant only a two-hour hike up to the pass. Halfway there they met Signor Terni and Professor Morone of Susa, who had climbed up to the pass from the Italian side, a vertical gain of about six thousand feet, and now were descending toward them.

Dr. Morone warned them that the weather ahead looked ominous. Dark clouds were billowing up from Italy, and it began to rain heavily. The members of our team turned back down the French side and joined us with Jumbo. It would have been miserable at the pass. Our decision to postpone Hannibal's speech encouraging his troops at this key point until another day turned out to be fortuitous. That "other day" has now become a tradition in which we team members and our extended families climb up to Hannibal's pass every five years, with the central event always being the delivery of Hannibal's speech by one of the original expedition members. In 2014, over thirty of us were there, and it was a particular joy to have my three-year-old granddaughter, Darcy, among the group.

On the way to the Mont Cenis pass meanwhile, Jumbo was completing her two-thousand-foot climb at such a rate that Ernesto and those of us hiking with her were exhausted. She didn't seem to be tired. Cattle grazing peacefully on the open slopes above tree level lifted their heads in surprise at the sight of Jumbo and then turned toward each other as their heavy Alpine bells tinkled. A full-spread photo of this scene in *Life* magazine shows snow-covered peaks in the background, two cows in the foreground, and three gendarmes behind Jumbo.

Within sight of the main motor road, we stopped for lunch near some whitewashed cottages. The Clapier team had now re-joined us, the rain had stopped, and along came the expedition truck with its provisions. Supplies were getting low by now, but Cynthia and Clare managed to find some food in the box, and Baldi brought water from a nearby well.

When everything was ready and the lorry packed, we woke Ernesto from his well-earned nap and set off toward the last two hairpin bends before the road curved over to the summit plateau. Just as we neared the second one, a little Italian car came racing down from the pass to pull up beside us. A moment later, Jumbo was waving her trunk joyfully as Signor Terni fondly patted her wrinkled cheeks and dropped sugar lumps into her mouth. To-gether, they stepped out resolutely. It was appropriate that Signor Terni, our generous sponsor and zoo owner, should lead Jumbo the last few hundred yards to the summit of the Col de Mont Cenis.

To the accompaniment of spontaneous cheers, Jumbo, her head held high, posed for photos behind the imposing sign reading: COL DE MONT CENIS. ALTITUDE 2,083 m.

Her great moment had arrived. After months of planning and preparation, we had achieved what seemed like an impossible dream. Two thousand years after Hannibal had so proudly told his men they had scaled the very ramparts of Rome, Jumbo waved her trunk in triumph as she looked past the border sign down into Italy, her home. From here, it would all be downhill. Our theme song became "Walking My Baby Back Home."

Over the ridge lay the Mont Cenis plateau with its lake and the ruined hospice Napoleon had founded. The lake was only five hundred feet away; we sauntered down the easy road in high spirits. It was the first time I had relaxed since the night march. The past few days had been heavy with problems and urgent decisions. But Jumbo had made it, and we had made it too. The way ahead was clear and life seemed full of bright horizons. The television photographers, newsmen, and others who had hailed the expedition excitedly at the summit headed down to Susa and their hotels.

We were joyful and finally at peace. As we walked, we chatted and joked. Ernesto was radiantly happy, and I sensed that his spirit had infected Jumbo as well. I asked him if I could have a ride, and he told Jumbo to stop.

"Leg up! Up, up, Jumbo. Stop!"

Jumbo lifted her left foreleg off the ground and held it so it looked like an enormous step. Ernesto told me to hold onto her ear and step up. I wondered if grabbing her ear would bother her, for I had to pull down on it with some force. Firmly grasping the edge of Jumbo's ear, I put my left foot up onto her leg and tried to hoist myself onto her back. It took two tries, but eventually I was astride—and feeling distinctly unstable.

"Put your knees behind her ears," shouted Ernesto. "That will keep you from sliding." Sure enough, that made all the difference; otherwise, I would have been in danger of sliding forward right onto her forehead. I let out a triumphant "Hey! This is great!"and asked, "Would someone please hand me my guitar?" For a few blissful minutes, I rode high on Jumbo playing my favorite flamenco music.

Hannibal had a favorite elephant, Surus, which he rode throughout his Italian campaigns. For a moment, I felt just a little like Hannibal. From eight feet up, the view was expansive. Below us lay the lake, glacial green-blue and calm. Around us mountains swept up toward snow-covered peaks. Life was good. I turned to God for a few minutes of quiet and thanks. As my heart welled up with joy, I was amazed at how easily a few thoughts of simple gratitude can be expressed. It was a moment to be treasured, a moment of exquisite joy.

After Cynthia and other members of the team also took rides to share the pleasure of the view, we arrived at a group of old, weather-beaten houses by the lake where we thought we might find shelter for Jumbo for the night. An obliging farmer willingly drove the tractor out of his barn to make room for her. All the way along, people had been generous to us, particularly in housing Jumbo. This was to be her highest-altitude night ever, and we did not want to risk her catching a chill.

Jumbo was safe and warm in her barn. Ernesto gave her a special banquet of carrots, oats, apples, bran, and sugar lumps to crown the day. Ernesto and Baldi were already happily installed in Jumbo's barn, enjoying free meals provided by the summit restaurant and surrounded by a cluster of excited Italians, mostly friends who had come up to greet them. They were listening to Baldi and Ernesto tell our spellbinding story over celebratory beverages.

Michael and Jimmy had motored down to Susa in the expedition car to get photographs enlarged for a commemorative album we planned to present to the mayor the next day. Last-minute thank-you ideas always complicated things, but eventually, they turned out well. Michael and Jimmy dined in Susa.

Most expedition members camped by the lake, a few minutes away. We were too tired to think of cooking and eating our dwindling food supplies. We wanted to celebrate. Five of us set off on foot to the one restaurant near the summit. We crowded noisily inside and sat down to the most magnificent dinner in celebration of Jumbo's achievement. Members of the press, by now friends, were there as well, so we made a loud and uproarious crowd. Strangely, there was no sign of our regular companion Stephen Barber, and I thought his absence odd.

It was pouring outside, and the night was pitch dark when we finally emerged from the restaurant. As the expedition car had not returned, we turned on the flashlights and walked back to camp. Our faces were lashed by the wind and heavy rain, our hair wetly swept back, but we were so joyful that the discomfort hardly mattered—until we found our camp completely drenched. Cynthia and Clare's tent leaked, and now the rain and wind had seeped in everywhere. Richard wanted to stick out the night in a tent. But Colonel Hickman, Clare, Cynthia, and I gathered up our sleeping bags and slipped and stumbled to the nearby farm.

We crossed the steep hummocky ground beside a swift mountain stream. Adjoining the farmhouse was a large barn divided into two parts. In one, several sturdy cattle were spending the night; in the other, we found mounds of soft hay piled high, which the farmer kindly made available for bedding. Here we settled in for sleep. Any discomfort or misery in getting to this point seemed inconsequential compared with the joy of having arrived "over the crest." For the first time in 2,177 years, an elephant had successfully summited the Alps along Hannibal's route. Tomorrow, we would cross the border into Italy. As I lay awake in my sleeping bag, soothed by the sweet smell of hay, I could not but be grateful that we had made the right decision about not taking Jumbo up to the Col de Clapier. Without the shelter that we were now enjoying, she and the rest of us would have passed the night in misery and danger. *Hannibal, when you reached the summit, you and your men were so exhausted you rested for two days. We are exhausted too, but are not going to wait, as the residents of Susa are about to give us the welcome of our lives!*

OVER THE TOP

> *Hannibal noticed that the men were in a state of low morale owing to all that they had suffered and would suffer, so he called them to a meeting and tried to cheer them up. He relied chiefly on the actual view of Italy. . . . he restored their spirits by showing them the plain of the Po.*
>
> —Polybius

Our tenth day dawned. The previous night, our camp at nearly seven thousand feet above sea level, had been cold—just above freezing. Michael and Jimmy had driven up late from Susa. The two of them and Richard survived the night, with its icy wind, in their tents, while the rest of us were relatively warm in the farmer's barn. Now the morning was bathed in sunshine and there was that exhilarating tang in the air that comes after a night of heavy rain. The early morning breeze, rising briskly from across the lake, tousled our hair as we prepared to start our downhill trek.

Now that we had reached the summit, the speed-time section of our logbook that kept record of our progress parallel with Hannibal's was closed. Our original plan had always been only to mimic and study the nine days of Hannibal's ascent. Nevertheless, as we set out from Jumbo's barn, I took readings and entered them in the logbook, which, by now, was dilapidated and damp. We were interested to see how Jumbo responded to the long, steady downhill descent.

The road ran along the side of the lake, past Napoleon's ruined hospice, and then to the edge of the Col de Mont Cenis plateau. From here we could survey the fine view of the surrounding mountains, but the Po valley was still out of sight. Only the Col de Clapier allows for the view that Polybius describes so clearly.

After a pause of a few minutes, we plunged downhill toward the frontier post, half a mile on. Jumbo's passport was a makeshift affair, thought up at the last moment and unnecessary, as Signor Terni had already arranged international travel papers for his elephant. However, we felt that Jumbo should have a proper, super-sized passport, so we came up with one, spontaneously. It had a white cardboard cover, taken from the bottom of a candy carton, and pages provided at the last moment by Alexandre, the French TV cameraman. Jumbo's passport was about a foot square; as we walked along, we had fun composing the information to be entered, then crowned the oversized passport with a photo of Jumbo.

At the Italian frontier post, Jumbo behaved beautifully. She handed her passport to the border guard for inspection. Playing his part well, he studied it thoroughly to confirm Jumbo's identity. The border guard stamped her passport with a great flourish and handed it back to her. At this point, a crisis arose, as Jumbo was about to eat the passport, but Ernesto managed to grab the valuable document first. Having lifted the border barrier with her trunk and posed for an increasing number of photographers, Jumbo passed on into her homeland—Italy.

We prepared for our celebration coffee party en route. We had been given an elephant-shaped cake back in England. One cannot possibly imagine anything more fragile and less necessary to a mountain expedition than a huge cake in a thin cardboard container. The cake had survived, barely. By the time the caravan arrived at the appointed roadside cafe, the proprietor, dressed in white apron and tall chef's hat, had worked miracles. Here was our poor benighted elephant cake, looking as good as new! Never was there a coffee party such as this! We sat in the sunshine with the chef beaming at us from his doorway and Jumbo's inquisitive trunk dangling down into the center of our celebration. She was clearly very interested in this cake, so much so that after a first serving with the help of her trunk, she insisted on a second piece before anyone else had had their first. We gladly agreed. After all, this was in her honor, but we made sure that at least some cake was available for the rest of the expedition members.

All seemed well with the world as we sauntered downhill toward Susa. Jumbo was on my right and Ernesto on my left. Ernesto was reading aloud the English translation of the day's edition of *La Stampa*. Evidently, so he read, the British Alpine Hannibal Expedition now appeared to be a fraud, badly managed, and unreliable. I grabbed the paper from him and ran my eye to the bottom of the front-page article. Who would possibly write such a report just when we were about to bring our triumphant elephant down the mountain? There, unmistakably, was the name of our most trusted reporter, Stephen Barber, who had been the official representative of one of our sponsors.

Only four nights ago, Barber had been sitting on Jumbo's jacket—which we had laid out to be our ground tablecloth—sharing supper with the team. We were on track with our itinerary, based on what we had hoped for and promised. Responding warmly to our hospitality, Barber had offered a toast to the expedition. We replied in the same spirit, with a toast to the *News-Chronicle*. Having been well-fed, Jumbo was patiently standing in the background, poised for the proposed photo shoot. The camera flashed, and the picture was cabled to London and New York. The photo would convey to the British public a happy campsite, a contented elephant, with wine flowing, good company, and much to celebrate. Now it seemed that Barber had undercut the integrity of the expedition.

I took his criticisms to heart. As leader, I felt humiliated, with a devastating sense of being vulnerable to unwarranted criticism. Naturally, I worried about what the public might now be thinking of our enterprise, and was aware that public opinion could easily switch from praise to criticism. This approach of attacking us via his own newspaper, the very one that was sponsoring us, was beyond any feared criticism.

There had always been the possibility that some untoward accident could be heralded to the world, completely changing our fortunes. Barber's story, translated into Italian, threatened to do just that, depicting our expedition as carnival-like and trivial. The person we trusted most outside the team had let us down. At least the column was so hot off the press that its claims would not yet have reached the joyful crowds awaiting us in Susa.

What would Signor Terni, our generous and most trusting patron, think of us? The report indirectly slighted him for entrusting his elephant to such a questionable team. Our sense of pride in the achievement now seemed premature and about to be deflated even before we were to arrive in Susa. How was I going to speak to Barber upon arrival?

The mayor had asked that we arrive at Susa at 6 p.m. We were well ahead of schedule, so stopped in the shade of some welcoming trees on a grassy slope to regroup and relax. Baldi produced a surprise bucket of carrots for Jumbo, and our team gathered on the grass. Ernesto gave us more details of Barber's article. We later found that the London editor of the *News-Chronicle* had deleted all the critical parts so that the British public read only good things about us. Unfortunately, *La Stampa* received the fuller version. Now that our team knew the situation, we agreed that this was not the time for recriminations. We would behave as graciously and courteously as possible to Barber and his wife. I remained troubled, though, knowing my own frailties and vulnerabilities.

A Finnish radio producer arrived and recorded interviews with the team. At odd moments since having crossed the Col, various microphones had been pushed in front of us for statements. An inkling of the kind of reception awaiting Jumbo was dawning. I was concerned over my nonexistent Italian. Fortunately, an interpreter from the mayor's office motored up to

Jumbo's triumphant arrival at Susa, Italy.

brief us on preparations. He was a youthful student, bubbling over with enthusiasm and continually referring to our evening's host as "My Lord Mayor." Together we composed a speech in Italian to thank the mayor for what would undoubtedly be a superb reception.

We set out for Susa, leaving a comfortable hour before the planned six o'clock arrival time, and saw what Jumbo could do on the gentle, steady decline. Her consistent four to five miles an hour made an unusual entry in the logbook. It was hard work stopping to enter the readings and then running to catch up.

Susa was completely jammed with people. Farm folk had come in from miles around. The population of the small city had swollen to three times its normal size. A huge banner spelling out "Welcome, Jumbo" was at the city entrance, and the crowds closed in around us. The mayor of Susa and Mr. Bateman walked up to meet us. We shook hands warmly. The mayor and I simultaneously smiled at the thought of our necessary speech-making.

Then came the dancers in their bright regalia, and the band playing at full volume. The excitement, animation, and enthusiasm of the milling thousands imprinted on my mind an image that I will never forget. Jumbo was made an honorary member of the Alpini, Italy's exclusive mountaineering club, with the ceremonial presentation of alpine hat and medal to be put around her neck by the local president. She was led to the cathedral square and fed with carrots from a bright orange machine. It was the pride of the town—a brand-new earthmover with the nickname "Jumbo" written in bold letters across its flanks.

Then came a great honor: Our elephant was solemnly led through the famous triumphal arch, which had been erected in 7 B.C. by King Cozeo for the Emperor Augustus, 211 years after Hannibal had passed that way. The procession proceeded to the town hall. While Jumbo was being taken through palatial gates to a courtyard where she could abide in complete luxury, we were whisked up to the mayor's parlor for speeches and presentations. Local dignitaries and members of the press crowded in.

The reception was magnificently and meticulously arranged. The mayor said his piece in English better than I did mine in Italian. Our speeches were well received and loudly applauded. Thanks to Jimmy's hard work the previous evening, we were able to present an album of expedition photographs to the mayor.

I had one final statement to make, so I called over our enthusiastic student interpreter to assist. It ran like this:

"Hannibal had crossed the Alps on a mission of death and destruction, literally in revenge for the defeat of his father and his country in the earlier war. We can admire his courage and leadership but not his mission of death and destruction. Could we not contrast that historic journey with Jumbo's which, we hope, has brought only celebration and friendship. One of the most unforgettable memories of the journey has been the light of joy on the faces of children and adults alike all the way along the route. But all is not peaceful today. The world lives under the threat of atomic warfare. Intercontinental ballistic missiles are the most pressing fear of the day. What was launched at Mont-mélian has now landed safely in home territory, a peaceful, intercontinental, Hanniballistic elephant!"

The speech was well received; a lot of that being due to our interpreter's putting full emotional expression into his translation.

We were now guests of the city. The comfortable hotel rooms seemed more than luxurious after nine nights of mountain camping. The joy of a hot shower was almost beyond words. After settling in, we strolled over to a restaurant on the other side of the central square to see ourselves on television. It was an extraordinary sensation to watch ourselves arrive in Italy. Things I had not noticed at the time now stared me in the face. There were details that made the day's events almost four-dimensional. A background shot showed a reporter pumping up his bicycle tire. An elderly couple was caught gazing with fascination at the elephant. It was particularly gratifying to see the expressions of joy on peoples' faces.

The reception banquet, hosted by the city, was magnificent. Afterward, we went for a moonlight stroll in the ancient Roman quarter. Most of us were too tired to take it all in but just enjoyed being alive and together, in the afterglow of the adventure. This was certainly a different kind of tiredness than that of the Carthaginian army, which Polybius described as being in "a wretched condition."

We slept until noon the next day and enjoyed a leisurely lunch and wonderful, strong Italian coffee at an outside cafe in the brilliant sunshine. As we discussed the previous day's splendid welcome, it became clear that not a word had been mentioned about Barber's article. In the midst of the celebration, Signor Terni had said to me as an aside, "Don't worry about the article. It will not make any difference." I passed this on to the others and began to soften my attitude. Time and success—with the addition of glory, no matter how unearned—have a way of healing wounds.

Jumbo was comfortable in the stable courtyard on the square opposite our hotel. When we visited her with Ernesto and Signor Terni, she looked content and pleased to see us. The Italian Society for the Prevention of Cruelty to Animals sent a representative veterinarian, who thoroughly examined Jumbo. He came out with a public statement that she was in excellent condition, and had lost two hundred pounds in weight, which was good for her. Naturally, it was wonderful news for us. Signor Terni decided that Jumbo should not have to walk the final twenty-five miles to Turin, and booked her passage on a train. She had a large covered-goods compartment all to herself; we followed the next day.

Jumbo now came home to Turin and the reception we received was completely different from Hannibal's. Jumbo was the ultimate heroine, coming back to her hometown like an Olympic gold medalist. There was an even finer, enthusiastic welcome by the Turin crowds than we'd seen in Susa. The Fiat band, the complete traffic disruption, and general cessation of all work downtown in that great city, until the famous *elephantessa* had passed by, all added up to a grand finale. This celebration was the biggest and best of all.

A hundred yards before the zoo gates, we persuaded Ernesto to mount Jumbo, whom he had so patiently led all those miles. He had walked every step of the way, and if anyone should share in the glory belonging to Jumbo, it was he. Through gates of splendor decorated with welcome signs, he rode her into the Giardino Zoologico. A great cheer went up from the crowd and the zoo workers. Ernesto's friends and Signor Terni hurried forward to welcome him as he dismounted. A brightly painted sign had been erected over the gates: "Casa Yumbo!" (Jumbo's home). With her head high, she eagerly made her way to the elephant pen, where a royal feast awaited her: two tables stacked with apples, bananas, oranges, and pears. Lady that she was, she paused patiently for a photo with the team before indulging. We can only say that Bella was a "happy camper!"

The welcome dinner in Turin was well-attended by dignitaries including the mayor and the British and French consuls. I sat between Mr. Bateman, the British consul, and a Roman senator, Senator Sibille, who had strongly opposing views on Hannibal's route, and with whom we had already had a long correspondence and now a lively conversation. He held to the theory that Hannibal had traversed three passes: the Col de Montgenèvre and the subsidiary passes of La Scalla and Bousson. No wonder Signor Terni, who arranged the lavish dinner, had us sit together. From across the table, his amused face was watching the glint of battle in our eyes. Two people from different countries and backgrounds can disagree with each other and yet thoroughly enjoy each other's company. Our discussion was long and lively, amid mild interjections from Mr. Bateman.

The end of the "contest" consisted of a warm invitation from the senator to visit his mountain chalet and have him personally conduct me over the three passes. While I accepted gladly, I remained unmoved by his theory. His proposed route provided no view of the Po valley, and the descent would have been too easy. Polybius's account is adamant on those two points.

After the banquet, the time came for presentations and speeches. We presented the mayor with an album of expedition photographs. Two oddly shaped parcels were brought forward and in due course handed to Signor Terni. The first contained Jumbo's famous passport and the other one of her boots. We felt now, as the finale of our drama was drawing to a close, that surely Signor Terni deserved the largest number of curtain calls. When Mr. Bateman had first called him about our planned expedition, he acted spontaneously and provided his elephant and Ernesto, the gifted mahout, free of charge. Also, knowing that we were supporting the World Refugee Year, he had provided Baldi, his truck, mules, petrol, train transportation, and enough food to keep Jumbo going for the complete twelve days.

Our last album of photographs was for Mr. Bateman. In the front was an illustrated parchment with the words: "To Mr. E.C. Bateman, with many thanks for finding us an elephant to take over the Alps in search of Hannibal."

My mind went back to the foggy December evening at the YMCA in Birmingham when, while waiting in line for supper, I first opened his letter: *I am happy to inform you that I have been able to secure an offer of an elephant for your projected crossing of the Alps . . . .*

Those were the words that launched the journey now drawing to its close. Under a star-studded sky, our team went over to the elephant stables to say good-bye to Jumbo. This was a journey she would never forget.

What about Stephen Barber? Looking at my journal notes for that evening, I had written: *All ended v. happily. Chatted gaily with Terni, Bateman & Senator. Shook hands with Stephen B. and wished him well. I think he could tell that we as a team had gotten over the incident in the light of Jumbo's achievement. Mrs. Barber kissed all the team with warm affection, as if she was the one to make the peace.* After all our elephant had done, Barber's article did not seem to make much of a difference.

What about Jumbo? She was back home in her stall. I can genuinely affirm that she had had a wonderful time. A year later when I visited her at the zoo, Jumbo clearly recognized me.

That last evening, we left her quietly munching her supper after we members of the expedition whispered sweet nothings into her big ears and asked her not to forget us. We could honestly say, as we went our different ways, that we would most definitely miss her. As had been our theme, our heroic pachyderm had indeed come home.

Green reflects the joy and challenge of crossing of the Alps with Jumbo. Afterward, my color scheme shifts to blue as I head out to the wide open spaces of the new world of the western United States.

Chapter 5

Silicon Valley and the Counterculture —My Journey into Light

The color here is blue—for the vast horizons of possibility and opportunity. It is often used to convey creativity and intelligence. Its wavelength is 455 to 497 nanometers.

> *Huck, you don't ever seem to want to do anything that's regular; you want to be starting something fresh all the time.*
> —Tom Sawyer, in *Adventures of Huckleberry Finn*, by Mark Twain

To Tell the Truth

January 1960, New York City: I glanced at my two fellow contestants sitting beside me and smiled self-consciously, knowing that the eyes of over 10 million viewers were upon us. Four months earlier, I'd been camped atop the French-Italian Alps with a two-and-a-half-ton elephant named Jumbo. Our team of explorers had sought the most likely path for Hannibal's legendary march on Rome in 218 B.C. Now, staring out in the glare of camera lights at the studio audience of a popular national television show, I wondered myself if I had really had that wild adventure in the Alps. Living such a grand dream now seemed as flimsy as gossamer, as unreal as the whole facade of the television studio where we were all now sitting.

A scant week earlier, I'd been a passenger on the SS *America* as it steamed past the snow-covered Statue of Liberty to Manhattan. I had prepared for my first visit to the United States—expecting to stay a couple of years or so and then return home—by reading *The Catcher in the Rye* on the six-day crossing, since a friend in England had suggested it as a good introduction to post-war America. I spent my first night in New York in a seedy downtown hotel. It was cold outside, the radiator heat was suffocating, and I couldn't open the window. I passed a restless night alternately sweltering, half naked on the bed, and dashing out onto the landing to cool off.

A couple of days later came the call from the television station. A woman's voice with a Southern accent said: "Mr. Hoyte, we have heard of your adventure, and we wonder if you would like to consider being on our 'To Tell the Truth' show?"

"Well, what does it involve?" I asked.

"A panel will guess if you are the person who took the elephant over the Alps." After a thoughtful pause, not knowing anything about American television but eager for a new experience, I accepted. The woman advised me to arrive at the studio "next Tuesday at 2 p.m., and we will get you prompted."

So began my first American adventure. On the show, there was to be a panel of three, one of whom had crossed the Alps with a pachyderm while the other two, having done their homework, would pretend to have led the two-week, hundred-fifty-mile expedition. Our journey had garnered significant media attention, including a seven-page spread in *Life* magazine, the biggest story that week. On the show, a panel of celebrities—actor Tom Poston, news commentator John Cameron Swayze, actor and writer Hildy Parks, and singer-actor Kitty Carlisle—would ask each of us questions about the adventure seeking to decide who was the real elephant rider.

One of our panel members, with an impeccable Oxford accent, was from the British embassy, while the other sold Rolls-Royce motorcars in the city and also sounded British. On the day before the live show, I sat down with them so we could get to know each other. I related the story of Hannibal and covered as many questions as we could anticipate. Who was General Hannibal? Why did his army cross the Alps? Why did he take thirty-seven elephants? How did I manage to get an elephant? How did I feed the elephant? What was I trying to prove? The two of them busily made notes which they would review overnight. I was expected to strictly tell the truth, but their goal was to pretend to be me and provide answers that sounded convincing, whether true or not. If we outwitted all four questioners, we would share $2,000; if three guessed incorrectly, we would share $1,500, and so on.

The next day, after "makeup" and "final protocol," it was show time. Vivid smells of sprays and ointments filled the makeup room. A light dusting of powder was applied so our faces would not look too shiny under the spotlights. A lot of cigarette smoke drifted around. The chatter was about the celebrities, though the makeup artist did ask as she worked on my face, "Did you really do it?" As we went onstage, I noticed an off-screen cheerleader whose job was to encourage an enthusiastic response from the two hundred people from off the street who made up the studio audience. He was wielding a sign that read, "Applause!" In one sense, it was all canned and surreal, yet there was a dynamic in the to-and-fro of questions and answers that was clearly appealing to the nationwide audience and to me personally. I was having fun!

"Who was the Roman general who finally defeated Hannibal?" the host asked the British consul. I held my breath. Could he remember our previous day's review of the facts?

He hesitated and I wanted to mouth the answer to him— but 10 million sets of eyes were watching us, including our lips, for any slip.

"Scipio," he replied. I exhaled, relieved.

The whole world seemed to be guessing who I was, and I realized that at a deep level, I wasn't quite sure myself. Finally, the questioning was finished, the celebrities had done their best to celebrate truth from lies, and our emcee asked: "Will the real John Hoyte please stand up?"

On cue, the three of us deliberately put our hands flat on the table we shared, leaning forward slightly—shifting in our chairs—as if any one of us might rise to his feet, or perhaps we really couldn't decide among ourselves who was the real John Hoyte.

But after a few long seconds of well-rehearsed, deliberate hesitation, there was a pushing back of my chair, a straightening of my knees, a feeling of utter exposure—almost nakedness—and then the inevitable, broad smile. Seemingly from a distance, I heard loud applause, chatter, and humorous expletives from the three panelists who had judged us wrong. For a moment, I was all alone. Then I was standing under the lights feeling foolish—playing a make-believe game in a make-believe world—yet triumphant that we had outwitted most of our questioners.

All except Tom Poston had guessed wrong. When asked why he chose me, he replied, "One eccentric can spot another." What did that say about me? Perhaps I did not look like the type of person who would take an elephant over mountains. Perhaps that was the point of the game: the dangers of stereotyping people.

What persona did I project to others? Eccentricity is an advantage if it challenges the status quo and helps people think "outside the box." On the climb, the media had hailed me as a Cambridge classics professor, a highbrow title that I attempted to deny. People love to pigeon-hole their heroes and put them on pedestals. I did my best to counter that, though I eventually took the compliment with a smile. But this was different. I had to stand up to the firing line which was the truth, the whole truth, and nothing but the truth.

My quest for a new kind of life sprang from that moment. This was more than just stuffing the whole game and its questions into my bag of memories of unusual experiences, and then moving on. As I now unstuff that bag fifty-some years later, I see this point in the quasi-Hannibal journey as crucial to discovering a deeper purpose for my life. Enough of elephants and Alps!

Though we would probably never see each other again, the three of us who had said we were John Hoyte parted with a special memory of this unique occasion—in addition to carrying away a check for $500!

And the question lingered in my mind: *"Will the real John Hoyte please stand up?"*

Who was the real John Hoyte? Yes, a leader of an Alpine expedition but also a young boy, one of six kids, in a close, missionary family in China; an orphan in a Japanese internment camp during World War II, an English schoolboy, and then a Cambridge student.

Now, who was I in this land across the sea? How was to find a new life with all the hard knocks and mixed joys of the past as ballast?

Finding My Bearings

After such an unusual beginning to my journey west, I felt ready for new experiences. Although I was now twenty-seven, this different world of the United States seemed so fresh and delightful to me that I felt like a schoolboy on an adventure. Seeing things, people, and events with such vividness and pleasure, I was constantly bowled over with surprises. I know this from rereading my journal from those early days. Vivid flashes of memory remain to this day.

> *A cold, brilliantly sunny morning in New Haven,*
> *Connecticut. Snow on the ground. Just below freezing. I*
> *am staying with Uncle Paul and Auntie Ruth, having*
> *taken the train from New York. They have gone off to*
> *work, and I have the run of the house. Have just*
> *discovered Brahms' Second Piano Concerto on their*
> *record player. I am bowled over.*

Walking out over the snow-blanketed landscape, I found the music enrapturing my soul and adding another dimension to the visual beauty. Everything seemed as clear as this crisp day, with the past and future coming together in one cohesive blend. It was a heady moment. Confidence is a strange thing. Nothing is wasted. All those experiences as a child and adolescent seemed to be cohering into a tangible substance. It suddenly appears: It is confidence.

A deeply sun-tanned man was standing on the New Haven railway station platform. I asked him where he could get so much sun in the heart of winter. His answer, with a smile, was *Florida*, only a two-hour flight south! I was immediately struck by the fact that the United States contains a wide range of climates, contrasted with the relatively small island of Britain, though the climate there seems to change every other day.

I visited Richard at Yale University. After our elephant trip, he was now a Ph.D. candidate in economics—and later would become deputy director of UNICEF and be knighted Sir Richard Jolly by the queen. We went over the Hannibal trip together, with its "if only's," "maybe's," and the many humorous twists. I put on his vinyl record of Verdi's *Requiem* and turned up the volume. We discussed the riches of Europe with its cultural beauties as we had shared them together. The music brought back memories of the trip to Rome after Jumbo's crossing, the splendid receptions, and Verdi's *Aida* in a huge open-air amphitheater. Of all my friendships from Cambridge, I found that my bond with Richard was unique and always will be. In the years to come, when visiting New York, I stayed with him and his family on Roosevelt Island, across the river from where he worked at the United Nations, as Alison, his wife, was on the way to becoming the world expert on the lemurs of Madagascar.

As I flew over the snow-covered Midwest, the vastness, the flatness, and the huge crisscross patterns of the winter fields took my breath away. It was all so new to me. I felt I was flying over another planet.

From Dungeness Spit on Washington's Olympic Peninsula, I watched the sun dip into the Pacific with my brother Eric and his wife, Virginia. They had just moved up to Seattle from San Francisco. Their newborn, Roland, was nestled cozily in a blanket in between the rocks at low tide. He and I were both starting new lives.

I took the Greyhound bus to San Francisco for my new adventure. Staying in Seattle with Eric and Virginia was a refreshing respite, but I was eager to find a job, a home, and a living. I had a master's degree in electro-mechanical engineering from Cambridge University but was unsure how much weight it would have out there. In addition, I had three years of experience in British industry and some unusually specialized leadership experience with our elephant expedition. I settled on the Bay Area because of its creativity and good engineering opportunities. The San Francisco Peninsula was already famous, with Stanford University being the inspiration and incubator for small, innovative companies. There would be no better place to start, I felt. My quest was to find a work environment emphasizing creativity.

As I climbed on the bus at the central station in Seattle, I had $800 saved up from England and my appearance on "To Tell the Truth," but I felt like a millionaire. The bus was almost full, so I couldn't get a window seat. I settled down as comfortably as I could for the eight-hundred-thirty-mile overnight ride, hoping to get some sleep. I took several sleeping pills, but they were not working. Reading my brother's Sierra Club magazine helped me pass the time. This was a new experience. In England, I would travel by train, car, bicycle, or hitchhiking but not by long-distance bus. Oh, if only I could put my feet up so that I could at least halfway lie down. The bus approached San Francisco via Berkeley and the East Bay, so we did not cross the Golden Gate Bridge. I was disappointed but on the other hand got a magnificent view of the bridge, the bay, and the city itself shining in the morning sun as we sped along the Berkeley freeway.

I took a taxi from the bus station to the YMCA on Turk Street. I had lived at the "Y" for three years in Birmingham and for the planning of our Hannibal expedition. This would be my home until I found a job. That first evening stays in my memory. It was clear and crisp, with none of the fog that rolls in during the summer. I walked the streets, took a cable car ride, hanging on by a foot and an arm, went down to Fisherman's Wharf, smelled the rich salt spray and crabs, and was enchanted. No wonder people around the world sing, "I Left My Heart in San Francisco."

Up in my sixteenth-floor room with its tiny desk, chair, bed, and mini-cupboard, I got out my journal and listed priorities: buy a car, get a job, and find a good place to live. It would be an adventure, a quest for meaning through creative work.

I was humming and muttering to myself *Get car, get car, get car* as if I were rooting for a football team as I took the elevator down to street level the next morning. The *San Francisco Chronicle* was for sale at the corner, and I retreated with it to the residents' lounge with its funky, old furniture and smells of tired old men and stale cigarette smoke. Then I scanned the auto ads.

Two days later, I was the proud owner of a 1953 Studebaker sedan. It had eighty thousand miles on the odometer, but for $300, what could I expect? At least the tires had good tread. Parking in the city was expensive and hazardous, so it was definitely time to move out for my job search.

Most engineering jobs were either down the San Francisco Peninsula or across the bay in Oakland or Berkeley. Fortune was kind to me. My brother Eric's wife, Virginia, had a sister, Sally, who lived in Menlo Park. I called her and was heading south the next day. Sally and Bob lived up in the hills behind Stanford University, another place I would love to visit, and I was warmly welcomed. They had two boys, ages eight and six, and a typical Californian ranch-type bungalow, spacious with lots of expansive windows and two magnificent live oaks overhanging the cedar shake roof.

Of the five thriving companies I was eying on the Peninsula, my application was accepted at Ampex, which made and developed tape recorders and a wide range of recording equipment; Hewlett-Packard, the up-and-coming leader in electronic measuring equipment; and Varian, which made specialized vacuum tube equipment. Evidently, English engineers had a good reputation in the West. After a big discussion with Sally and Bob, I chose Hewlett-Packard, starting work in April. The choice was fortuitous considering the future of the five companies. This was not yet Silicon Valley. Though all five had a part to play in its development, Hewlett-Packard was the leader.

After knocking on many doors, I found a furnished place to live in the neighboring town. The newspaper listing read:

IN LOS ALTOS. 1½ blocks from Main St., large,
comfortable, studio apt.
Gar. & util incl. Employed gentleman preferred.
$85.00 per month.

It was one of the oldest homes in Los Altos, with a huge veranda surrounding the ground floor, whitewashed, three stories high, and surrounded by a jungle of a garden, mainly pepper trees. The owner matched the house: an elderly, white-haired gentleman with hearing aid, dark blue suit, waistcoat, and pince-nez glasses. It all seemed far from modern California, more like a glimpse of a settled early-twentieth-century world. I was hooked by the ambiance and the spacious upstairs rooms, and was particularly partial to pepper trees.

As a bonus, I made immediate friends with Bob Martin, an engineer who had the apartment below me. That first week, on a balmy evening, we sat on the swing bench on the veranda and discussed our lives. We found that we shared the same spiritual values, a sense of wonder at existence, and particularly the wonders of nature. He had just gotten a job with Fairchild Semicon-

ductor, a three-year-old startup company. I remarked that I was
interested in classical music, and the early Elizabethan period in
particular. Bob offhandedly said that his boss, Bob Noyce, was
director of a local choral group, the Palo Alto Madrigal Singers.

The following Wednesday, I arrived at a bungalow in Palo
Alto to meet nine other singers. Within minutes, I was singing
"The Silver Swan," one of my favorite madrigals. This amazed
me. Here I was, having come over six thousand miles only to
find brilliant scientists and innovators who were also well
versed in the ultimate English choral style—the unaccompanied
madrigal!

I chatted with Bob Noyce over end-of-evening refreshments.
He was very modest, sight-read music brilliantly, and sang bass.
I learned that he was one of eight engineers who had left William
Shockley's firm three years earlier and was now a founder of
Fairchild Semiconductor. Shockley, a Nobel laureate, was co-in-
ventor of the semiconductor back in 1954 but had lost the eight
employees because he was an ineffective administrator.

Bob went on to be the inventor of the integrated circuit, co-
inventor of the microprocessor, and founder and president of
Intel. Meeting him brought me back full circle to my time teaching electronics in the British Army when I originally heard about
the invention of the semiconductor, the basis for everything else
that has happened in Silicon Valley, and wondered if I might have
a part to play in its coming development. Now I had met someone who was at the very heart of this revolutionary new world.
I felt privileged.

Several other members of the singing group were working
with Bob or were related to the founders of his company. Jea-
neen was the wife of Charlie Sporck, founder and president of
National Semiconductor, and Rose was the wife of Eugene
Kleiner, one of the original eight engineers and a founder of
Kleiner-Perkins, the premier venture capital provider for many
of Silicon Valley's most successful enterprises. I firmly believe

that there is an integrating loop between scientific innovation and the musical arts. Creative, imaginative people very often round out their lives with participation in some form of the arts, frequently music.

We met in each other's homes every week, a group that would come to mean much to me over the years. It certainly eased my transition to the American West Coast lifestyle. The group is still going, over fifty-five years later, and I still sing with them if I am visiting Palo Alto from my home in Bellingham, Washington. I remember the night that Bob mentioned, almost nonchalantly, that he was leaving Fairchild, which did not have the resources to realize the potential of newly invented silicon chip, and starting a new company to be called Intel.

As I sipped hot tea, I remarked that it sounded rather like a telephone company. He replied, *Well, yes, but it is going to be called Intel anyway!*

We singers followed his exploits with interest. Then the night came when he told us he had developed what he would call the integrated circuit. His comment was, *And it is going to change everything!*

How well I remember that moment and the questions it raised. What changes does this mean? Of course, it is not going to change who we are and what the ultimate purposes of life are, but now, over fifty-five years later, I can see some of the profound changes Bob's invention brought: I go into my study after breakfast and check my email, make sure my iPhone is charged, and check the calendar on my iPad. I can Skype my sister in New Zealand and chat for an hour free of charge. The GPS in my car will direct me to anywhere I want. The integrated circuit and microchip have brought about profound changes. In many ways, life has become richer, with more information available and a new ease of communication. But there will always be the dark side. We can easily be drawn away from direct contact with people, nature, and the "real world" beyond technology.

A few years later, I arrived at Bob's home up in the hills behind Palo Alto for our annual madrigal Christmas party. I had my guitar in hand. We sang some carols and tried out the hand bells the Noyce family had recently acquired. When it was time for the children to go to bed, I sat on the staircase with my guitar and sang them the "Gnu Song," by the British comedians Flanders and Swann, then bade them good night. It was all such a complete family time, and everyone joined in the chorus: *O Ga-no, Ga-no, Ga-no, I'm a Gnu.* It didn't matter that Bob and others there were about to become multimillionaires while some of us, myself included, were struggling with startups and wondering how to pay the rent. We were *the family*, and the musical arts bound us closely.

At Home With Hewlett-Packard

Hewlett-Packard Corporation started in a garage in Palo Alto in 1939. Both Bill Hewlett and David Packard had graduated from Stanford University in electrical engineering under the mentorship of Professor Fred Terman, a brilliant educator who saw the potential in the two graduating seniors. Terman is considered the Father of Silicon Valley. The two young engineers' first product was an audio-oscillator, which their first customer, Walt Disney, needed in recording the sound track for his movie *Fantasia.* To understand Hewlett-Packard is to understand the birth of Silicon Valley and the principles of creative engineering that led to its success. The other key factor was the advent of the semiconductor.

The memories of my early days at Hewlett-Packard are vivid, marked by two sensations: The atmosphere was very relaxed and informal, quite the opposite of British industry with its strict structure and rigid hierarchy, and performance expectations were high but implied firmly and gently, not demanded. Trust was the basis for the company's smooth operation. There was trust in the products made, in fellow workers, and in management. Engineers were expected to be creative and innovative.

The company was growing rapidly. When I joined, it had nearly a thousand employees; in two years, there would be six thousand. That was the exciting environment I had landed in, and I considered myself fortunate. We produced electrical measuring and analytic instruments, and excelled in developing high-quality products with unique designs.

My first job was as a production engineer, with a desk in a large open area. I found that engineers were highly esteemed, and almost immediately, my ideas were listened to and could be effective. The open floor area was designed to encourage versatility and easy communications. If there was a hierarchical structure between management and ordinary engineers like me, I did not see it on the floor. Ralph Lee, vice president of engineering, had a desk in the middle of the floor just like mine, and he was most approachable for sharing simple pleasantries, discussing what we did over the weekend, or with an idea for improving a product. The fact that he was so approachable struck me as amazing and an eloquent sign of why our company was doing so well. I already called the company *ours*. The sense of part-ownership was quickly acquired. I found a huge emphasis on innovative engineering, and because of that, new products were coming out continually. A high percentage of the company's income was reinvested in research and development.

During my six years at "hp," as we called it, I had varied, interesting jobs. After my first assignment, I became a product engineer, which involved taking an idea, building a small team around it, working out the production bugs, and finally handing it over to full production. The wonderful thing about the job was that it required a combination of technical knowledge, manufacturing knowledge, and personnel skills. All of those provided excellent training for starting my own company, even though at the time, I had no expectation of that happening.

My first product was a line of high-precision, wire-wound resistors to be used in our new line of digital voltmeters, modestly claimed to be the most accurate in the world. Glen Weberg, my most companionable technician, and I set up shop in the old Redwood Building, the first building Bill and Dave had after the garage became too small. We formed a team of five and were able to develop a unique product which went into full production within six months. I was awarded a patent for designing a special silicon rubber bobbin onto which nickel-chromium wire was wound. It was a simple idea but provided stable resistors that do not change in value over time. Stability in a world of changing environments is highly prized by scientists. It was my first patent, and I had it framed.

I also learned that good ideas do not have to be complicated. The best ideas were often simple ones. Mathematicians and physicists are constantly looking for the simplest solution to a problem. A solution's beautiful simplicity can confirm its validity. This is one of the mysteries of mathematics and physics and, for me, points to a God of beauty and imagination.

My next project was much more complicated. Don Hammond, a brilliant scientist and physicist, had invented a quartz sensor that responded to changes of temperature in a remarkable way. It could change in frequency by a thousand hertz (cycles per second) for every one-degree centigrade change in temperature, giving us the most sensitive and accurate thermometer in the world. The problem was how to manufacture it reliably. This involved an elaborate vacuum chamber, quartz crystal slicing machines, minute assembly tools, and a lot of patience. Eventually, we got it right, and the finished product became a temperature standard for science labs around the world. However, as much as we tried, we could not bring down the price, so this specialty thermometer cost $3,000. Clearly, it was never going to be a best seller, but it found a home in some of the most sophisticated research and standards labs around the world. And the thermometer satisfied one of hp's aims: to make a significant contribution.

There were some remarkable characters at hp. Barney Oliver was the vice president of research and development. I was dating Astrid, a beautiful actress who was a close friend of his wife, who was also into drama. We had occasional stimulating evenings at the Oliver home, discussing everything from astrophysics to religion. Barney was a man of considerable influence and was pushing for government funds to set up a listening station for extraterrestrial life. He was a founder of SETI and Project Cyclops, a huge desert array of radio dishes used to listen for signs of extraterrestrial intelligence. Also, as Barney was an adamant atheist and I am a follower of Jesus, we had lively discussions, amicable but intense. He was one of a kind, widely read, a brilliant physicist, a great humorist, and a unique personality. I prized his friendship.

I got to know Bill Hewlett, mainly through our mutual interest in art. He had a unique collection of Japanese woodcuts, which I saw in his office but, naturally, were not available for general display. A long corridor from our engineering building to the corporate offices had blank walls. Since one of my long-term dreams was to blend art and science, I suggested to the personnel department that we show paintings by employees there. Six months passed, and nothing was done. I envisioned Bill's woodcuts hanging in the corridor's natural gallery, so I approached him about it. He responded enthusiastically, and before long, crowds of employees were walking the corridor admiring his collection. Goodwill about me seemed to be going from the personnel department to the top, judging by Bill's responsiveness when I asked him about the woodcuts. What was gratifying is that from that time on, hp had a permanent art gallery. We may have been the first company on the Peninsula to have one, but a whole industry has now grown up to provide works of art for companies in their Silicon Valley offices. Scientists need art to keep them sane, and artists have benefited from the financial support of scientists. Today's iPhone is an example of how the two have joined, with its combination of simplicity, beauty, and functionality.

SPECTREX—MY JOURNEY FURTHER INTO LIGHT

As I left England, Dad had suggested I contact Uncle Fred upon arrival in California. He knew little about Fred Vreeland except that he had married my mother's sister Elizabeth, and that they lived in Mill Valley, just north of the Golden Gate Bridge. I looked up the name in the telephone directory and called. A cultured lady's voice responded with a gracious English accent. It was my Aunt Elizabeth.

Yes, do come up. Fred and I would love to see you and hear all about you and the family in England.

Theirs was an old redwood house, up a flight of slippery wooden steps in a steeply sloping redwood grove. Aunt Elizabeth was loving and welcoming. She was in her early eighties. Uncle Fred was ninety-two and used two walking sticks. He said, *John, come see my invention,* and took me down to the basement. There on a bench, among cobwebs and bric-a-brac, was a strange-looking instrument about eighteen inches square. A moment later, there was a flash, and I was afraid my uncle was going to electrocute himself. He unsteadily pointed me to an eyepiece, and when I looked through it, I saw a wonderful pattern of bright, colored lines. He explained that this was what he called a direct reading spectroscope. It could analyze the basic elements in any solid substance. He held the patent but was too old to develop the instrument into a marketable product. He wondered if I would be interested. It seemed that I could not get away from light and its beauty.

Two years later, I still had not taken him up on his offer. I visited again, and he gave me his engineering drawings. I found that Uncle Fred was not an easy man to deal with. Aunt Elizabeth explained that he was badly burned financially back in the early 1900s, and remained bitter and disillusioned. A brilliant scientist and inventor, he held the 1906 patent for a device that could create "undamped and sustained electrical oscillations," the first alternating electrical current source. She told me that, sadly, the Radio Corporation of America had stolen the patent for it, as well as several others of the thirty or so Fred had. He would not compromise when it came to his treasured ideas, and so had lost all his significant patents. Now, at the end of his life, Uncle Fred was bitter and resentful, while dear Aunt Elizabeth was gentle and gracious, a striking contrast.

I decided to try my hand at Uncle Fred's invention. It meant working on his spectroscope idea evenings and weekends and spending any savings I had on paying a local machine shop to manufacture two units. Seeing the economic potential of Fred's scientific device marked the first inklings of the entrepreneurial spirit within me. There was an advantage in being single at that stage of life.

But my social life was suffering, and Astrid headed to New York. It was a sad moment, but I was entranced by this other love: the brilliant colors of the visible spectrum and the possibility of being an entrepreneur. I plowed all of my discretionary income into the idea. At last, a device was complete, and I drove up to Sausalito, where Uncle Fred was in a nursing home. He was in his late nineties and suffering from dementia, sitting out in the garden in a wheelchair, hardly able to speak. He recognized me as I put my achievement proudly onto his blanketed lap. He slowly felt it in silence with his trembling hand. A tear ran down his cheek. He slowly realized that his final invention was now viable. I kissed him on the cheek and knew it was a moment to relish. This was the last time I would see him.

Thus began a totally new phase of life. I call it my journey into light. When I was in high school in England, I struggled with chemistry but loved physics. That led me to a study of light, which helped me get good grades in the final physics exam and a place at St. John's College, Cambridge. Now at Hewlett-Packard, light seemed to lead the way. My friend Charlie Reis had a small lab close to my desk, and was quietly doing research on a new kind of light source. He called it a "light-emitting diode." All I saw were little buttons of light on his lab bench. I saw him more as a friend than an inventor, but inventor he was, and in 1966, our company produced the first commercially available light-emitting diode. Now it has been developed into a huge industry, and most flashlights and traffic lights are LEDs, using far less energy than other sources of light.

I followed this trail from light-emitting diodes to light-emitting arcs, which were the basis for my new acquisition from Uncle Fred, the Vreeland Direct Reading Spectroscope, which could distinguish elements by the pattern of lines when a sample was vaporized and the light split into its component colors. Uncle Fred's patent was valid for eight more years. My immediate boss, Don Hammond, and I set up an appointment and demonstration for Bill Hewlett, with the possibility that hp might take over the spectroscope and make it one of its standard products, for uses such as in geology where analyzing unknown elements often was essential.

In a three-page proposal, I suggested that this could be the beginning of a new line of optical instruments for the company. One market I mentioned was higher education. Sputnik had been launched a few years earlier, and the U.S. government was funding technical education at universities and community colleges. The spectroscope was ideal for teaching geology and inorganic chemistry. The demonstration went well, and Bill Hewlett was clearly impressed. But after a couple of months of discussion with the marketing and manufacturing departments, he decided not to go ahead with the product. I was not sad but excited. Having given my employer the option of taking it over,

I felt at ease when I then asked: *Do you mind if I give it a go my-self?* The answer came back, *Good luck, John!*

I was able to leave hp with management's blessing and the assurance that if I could not make it, there would be a welcome mat for me back at my old job. I placed an ad in the *Geotimes* journal and received my first order for a spectroscope from George Fair, senior geologist at the U.S. Geological Survey in Washington, D.C. It was a good omen. This was a moment of joy as I flew to Washington and I hand-delivered the instrument to George on the fifth floor of the Naval Weapons Building. Nothing is more satisfying than making something that will be immediately appreciated. George showed me a large room piled to the ceiling with rock samples that needed to be sorted quickly. My spectroscope was ideal for this kind of analysis.

I left hp in April 1966 and established the Spectrex Corporation, a name suggested by John Chognard of the hp legal department, and it stuck. *Spec* stands for the spectra of light and *rex* for king. "We are the top of the line for spectroscopes!"

To this day, I marvel at the gracious treatment I received from the management at hp. They could have been unhappy with the fact that one of their engineers had been working on the side on a product that might be affecting his performance on the job. On the contrary—reflecting their general attitude toward engineers with innovations—they encouraged me. Bill Hewlett's approach was to help me along as much as possible. No wonder I was so impressed with his company.

After its start in the Menlo Park garage, Spectrex was housed at the back of Howard Bennett's machine shop. A gracious and understanding landlord, he undertook to handle all the machining for the spectroscope, and I flourished under this new arrangement. It was an exciting move from the garage to the new three-room space, and I took on my first employee. Keith Hollenbeck was Howard's son-in-law, skilled in both mechanical engineering and the new computers. I was a lucky man, and could spend more time marketing while Keith assembled the spectroscopes. Slowly, the orders increased, and we added some new products, including a line of miniature electronic pumps.

Fred Ottoboni, an employee of the state environment department whom I had met at a conference, turned up to show me his latest idea. From his briefcase he took a small cardboard box into which he had inserted one of our pumps.

"John, could you make us an air sampler which could be fitted onto a belt and worn by an industrial hygienist? We need to monitor the air in factories for safety and don't have anything available."

Excitedly, Keith set to work designing the first "personal air sampler" on the market. This led to forty years of air sampling products, with the present one, a little larger than a pen, fitting into a shirt pocket to monitor benzene, a carcinogen, at oil refineries. The day came when we received an order for twenty spectroscopes for the technical colleges of Taiwan. This was a huge order for our tiny outfit, now grown to seven employees.

My daughter, Lisa, showing off our latest product at the time, a Laser Particle Counter, 1974.

Today, looking west across the San Juan Islands and watching the setting sun emblazon the silky blue skyline, I look back with gratitude—to Uncle Fred and his unique product waiting to be discovered down in his basement; to Hewlett-Packard for giving me six good years of experience, rich with variety, ideal in preparing me to start and run my own company; and for the team we had at Spectrex as we weathered economic storms and emerged stronger each time. The prison camp experience in China, boarding school in England, two years in the military, and the elephant trip all played a role in the journey that has brought me to this point.

Moving from a large corporation to starting one's own venture was like transferring from being a petty officer on an ocean liner to owning a sailboat. It was an entirely different challenge. On the liner, there is the stability and the complex responsibilities of officers and crew within the structure. In one's own little sailboat, life, in a sense, is both much simpler and more demanding. The main object is to stay afloat and move in the right direction. You have to pay attention to every wave and shift in the wind. As you add crew members, you need to make sure each one pulls his or her weight. Bringing aboard the wrong person makes a huge difference and could even tip the boat over, while for the liner, with its levels among the crew, that person might fit better in another slot.

To me, the huge difference is the challenging demand for creativity and resourcefulness that the small-boat captain faces. Finally, the sense of achievement and satisfaction at the end of the journey is a high reward. I discovered that I am an entrepreneur at heart, an ideas man, an instigator, with all the problems this can bring. Ideas come flooding into my conscious mind, and of course, most of them go nowhere. The challenge is to move past those and put the others to work in ways that make a contribution to life, and to bring other people to see the same vision.

Silicon Valley is famous for its millionaires and successful start-ups. But for every success story, there are at least fifty companies that either go bankrupt or lose control of how their business is run to investors. In fact, the thinking in the Valley is that a startup either closes its doors within three to five years or grows rapidly. Through its fifty years, Spectrex has been proving that there is a third way. Stay small and manageable, remain profitable, avoid long-term debt to banks or venture capital firms, and maintain an atmosphere of creative enterprise. That was what we tried to do, and it seems to have worked—a deeply satisfying conclusion. Tim Jackson's book, *Prosperity Without Growth,* has presented a challenge to our Western way of thinking about economics. It points out that growth is not necessary to obtain reasonable prosperity. Moreover, it is becoming clear that the ecosystems that sustain our economies are collapsing under the impact of rising consumption and populations. The challenge is to develop a path to prosperity that doesn't depend on continued growth. Small, innovative companies can lead the way.

Light on the Mountain

> *Make no little plans. They have no magic to stir men's blood.*
>
> —Daniel Burnham

I was one of a group of engineers who were members of the Sierra Club. We enjoyed climbing in the Sierra Nevada, the magnificent range of mountains running north and south through almost the full length of California. John Borgsteadt, another engineer and close friend, and I set ourselves a challenge: to climb a different Sierra peak each year. Through this annual climbing expedition, I discovered the magic of the mountains, its range of light. John Muir, who persuaded Congress to make Yosemite a national park in 1890, became my hero.

In the summer of 1962, we got to the summit of Mount Hoffman, in Yosemite National Park, and found the Sierra Club logbook protected in a watertight, aluminum container. We read:

This mountain was first climbed in 1863 by Professor Whitney, from Harvard University, and his team of geologists.

We thought in amazement that that was right in the middle of the Civil War. I discovered later that the State of California had asked Professor Josiah Dwight Whitney to make a complete survey of its land. Mount Whitney, the highest peak in the contiguous United States, is named after him. The team must have been great mountaineers as well as geologists, for they were the first climbers known to have scaled the highest peaks in the Sierra. Professor Charles Hoffman was one of Whitney's team. We proudly signed our names in the logbook. On the way down, scrambling across a vast, steeply sloping field of scree, we realized that the coming summer of 1963 would be exactly one hundred years since the first climb.

What could we do to commemorate the 1863 event? The idea came quite quickly. One of us speaks out with imagination: *How about a series of beacon flares signaling from peak to peak from Mount Whitney in the south to Yosemite in the north?*

The other of us chimes in: *Wasn't that how the fall of Troy was signaled in ancient Greece, and how England was warned of the arrival of the Spanish Armada?*

The idea of reliving history catches our imagination. Ideas have legs and, as we hiked back to our campsite in Tuolumne Meadows, a possible plan took shape. In four weeks, we sent a letter out to all Sierra Club climbing groups in California listing the highest Sierra peaks and asking for volunteer leaders to choose a peak and be on its summit on the Sunday night of the upcoming Labor Day weekend.

Taking the courage of our convictions we write: *We the organizers of The High Sierra Centennial Climb, (John Borgsteadt, Doug Hayward, and John Hoyte) would provide flares and coordinate the operation.*

It was an act of faith, as we really did not know what would be involved. After we sent out the letter, I look at John and Doug, who was handling the administrative aspects of our project, and said ruefully, *It's easy to promise the flares, but where do we get them and how do we distribute them to our climbing leaders?*

After a feverish hunt and many phone calls, we found the Red Devil Fireworks Company willing to not only provide the green flares (green for peace) but also deliver them to John's home in Palo Alto. We were able to send sets of seven flares to each climbing group.

We had twenty volunteer climbing parties ready to ascend the twenty highest Sierra peaks so as to be on the top on the night of September 1. The weather was perfect, with a full moon flooding the mountain range. The first flare was to be lit at 9 p.m. on Mount Whitney, with the other flares lit from peak to peak at minute-and-a-half intervals, with the final one on Half Dome. That would signal the famous Fire Fall, the annual tipping over the edge at Glacier Point of burning embers from a huge bonfire, making a spectacular fall of fire visible from all over Yosemite Valley.

My group included three other climbers, Kent, from hp, George from Fairchild, and Joyce Dunsheath, leader of the British Women's Himalayan Expedition of 1956, who was visiting California on vacation. The Sierra Club had told her about our plan and, although in her late sixties, she wanted to join us. We found that our initial plan to climb Mount Darwin would require ropes, which we were not prepared for, to cross a dangerous stretch of the ascent. In a last-minute change of plans, we settled on Mount Tom, which still was more than thirteen thousand feet above sea level. But we were behind schedule and needed a full day of nonstop climbing to reach the summit by 9 p.m. Kent and George experienced altitude sickness, so Joyce and I had to leave them three-quarters of the way up. The two of us were still climbing at 8:45 p.m. We were completely exhausted and nearly desperate. Would we get to the summit in time?

Our flares on Cloud's Rest, Mount Lyle, and Half Dome—with moonlight on its south side.

We reached the jagged summit ridge as darkness fell, with only a few minutes to spare. It is a knife edge, and over that edge is a three-thousand-foot precipice! The lights of the town of Bishop, nearly ten thousand feet below, twinkled up at us. It was an ecstatic moment. After climbing doggedly in the near-darkness up the steep, craggy ascent, the wonder of reaching our goal in this surprise instant brought a moment of exquisite joy. The combination of relief that we were on time to light our flares, the experience of being able to stop climbing and rest our weary limbs and the beauty of range upon range of moonlit mountain peaks was almost too much to take in. It was a moment to relish. Having thrown off our backpacks, we stood in complete silence, awestruck, feeling a sense of wonder and vast love enveloping all the universe.

At 9:10, we saw a flare twenty-five miles south on North Palisade Peak. We saw another flare south of us and prepared to light our own. A minute later, our first flare was burning, and

Mount Abbott to the north took up the signal. Another flare, on Mount Ritter, was very faint. Unrolling our sleeping bags wedged between ledges of summit rock, under a brilliant full moon, we slept fitfully with discomfort but with deep satisfaction. This was my first opportunity to conceive of an expedition since the journey with Jumbo over the Alps. Sleeping on or near the summit of a mountain is dangerous if there is lightning around. It was with relief and much joy that on our return to civilization, we found that the whole enterprise was a success, with nobody in danger or hurt. I also have had the pleasure of meeting, at Sierra Club meetings discussing the flares, Ansel Adams, the famous naturalist and photographer; David Brower, president of the Sierra Club; and Frances Farquhar and Jules Eichorn, well-known mountain climbers after whom peaks have been named.

The Counterculture—Light Into a New World

I was living in the ferment of the Beat, Free Speech, the New Age, and the politically radical movements of the '60s and '70s but with wide, English eyes, willing to take in everything.

Mostly on the fringes, I was able to get involved to some extent in each of those movements, and became the wiser for it. From 1960 to 1965 were the bohemian years. Jack Kerouac and Allen Ginsberg led the way, Kerouac with his classic *On the Road* and Ginsberg with his poetry. We engineers and technical folk from the Stanford/Palo Alto area came up to San Francisco for weekends, and grew to love the interesting contrast with our middle-class lives.

Charlie, a friend from Palo Alto, suggested that I read Kerouac's other famous book *The Dharma Bums.* I couldn't put it down and found it eloquently portraying the lifestyle. Herb Caen of the *San Francisco Chronicle* coined the word "beatnik." Beat could mean several things: *Beaten down* or oppressed, the *beat* of their music or, as Kerouac would prefer, *Beatitude*. The Beats fit the older, established term, *bohemian*. Along with writers and artists, some of us "techies" were attracted to this unconventional life. I was ready to taste it for myself.

My introduction to bohemian friends in San Francisco was through my brother Eric and his wife, Virginia, before they moved to Seattle. Their good friends, Peter and Fox King, lived on Telegraph Hill, the center for the culture. They enjoyed free and easy bohemian living along with earning reasonable salaries. People drifted in and out of their pad, and were always welcomed. Wine was served, but there was no hard liquor and no drugs. I found this a refreshing contrast to the middle-class lifestyle of Palo Alto, and, because of Eric and Virginia, I was completely welcomed.

We were friends of a more way-out bohemian, Varda, a wonderful, older Greek, bearded and looking like Hemingway, who lived on a houseboat in Sausalito, across the Golden Gate Bridge and owned an Arabian dhow. We went out sailing. The craft was old, big, and clunky. Speed meant nothing. The joy was being out there, with all the new fiberglass yachts whizzing by while we enhanced the sailing scene in a grand relic from the past, noble in its heavy acacia construction. It was the ultimate bohemian gesture.

We enjoyed being together, living the simple lifestyle, enjoying nature, and resisting the onslaught of what appeared as soulless technology. There were poetry evenings, spontaneous dancing, and sitting on the carpet cross-legged discussing philosophy. Most of my friends in the city were artists or writers. Peter lectured on French literature at the University of California in Berkeley. Fox was a novelist. I thought that as an engineer, I might not fit in. But I was heavily into pen-and-ink sketching and flamenco guitar, as well as being the author of a published book *Alpine Elephant: In Hannibal's Tracks*—and was Eric's brother—so I was welcomed warmly. "Cool" endured. Perhaps I tried to convey to my new friends that the engineering world of the Peninsula was not so bad. I was delighted to live in both worlds; the contrast was invigorating.

San Francisco was an especially cool place in the early '60s. Though they come later, there were no sex parlors on Broadway and plenty of friendly cafes and jazz studios in town. The best was on Turk Street: the Modern Jazz Workshop, better known as the Black Hawk Studio. Dave Brubeck, Miles Davis and Thelonious Monk would play there. I would sit in a dark corner and sketch the players. Sketching was my way of absorbing the cool atmosphere. To my delight, there were three great flamenco bars. Pablo, an excellent teacher, came down the Peninsula once a week to give two of us flamenco guitar lessons. La Mariquita taught flamenco dance, and had a dance studio at the back of her Atherton home. I took lessons—and wore the right outfit.

This was a very happy stage of my life, with no family or financial commitments and a world of art, literature, music, and culture to explore from my base in Palo Alto. As an act of sheer extravagance, and because gas was 25 cents a gallon, I bought a used Thunderbird convertible in excellent condition. The contours were smooth and aerodynamic, the top was raised and lowered automatically, and the V8 engine was so quiet as to be almost inaudible. Nothing seemed more pleasurable than cruising along the coast road or up in the Santa Cruz Mountains. It was effortless and a sheer delight, but eventually, I replaced it with a sturdy old Volvo. My friends at hp teased me, parking in San Francisco was difficult, and it was out of tune with the bohemians. I had an amicable parting with Astrid.

Though the beatniks of San Francisco tried to continue their lifestyle, the Vietnam situation was deteriorating. The changes it made in the lives of many young people were changing the whole tenor of the Bay Area. I did not go up to the city as much, understandably as I had become interested in Alma Polinsky, a beautiful Canadian nurse at Stanford Hospital. Her family had fled from Kiev, in the Ukraine, back in the 1920s to escape the terrors of Stalin. What particularly struck me, apart from her beauty, was her adventuresome spirit. In 1962, she and five nursing friends had rented a VW bus and driven all around Europe. Their adventures fascinated me. I could see that she had a gracious manner but also a strong sense of courage and commitment. I was beginning to date her seriously when, in 1964, she decided to take off from her nursing career for six months and stay at a tiny village high in the Swiss Alps to study with Dr. Francis Schaeffer and his wife, Edith. Dr. Schaeffer, a noted philosopher and Christian thinker, had started a community and outreach for young people caught up in the counter culture. It was called *L'Abri*, French for *The Shelter.* Before she left, Alma explained to me that she was looking for clearer and more practical answers to her journey of faith. I admired her for that, and as we lightly kissed on the way to the airport, something was born in me that was beautiful—the beginnings of love.

While Alma was off in Switzerland on her journey of inner discovery, I was experiencing the beginnings of the counterculture. Springing from the beatnik world, the Free Speech Movement began in 1965 across the bay at the University of California in Berkeley, mainly over anger with the government's policies in Vietnam. Students protested a ban on campus political activities, demanding the right to free speech and academic freedom. Their actions were fueled by vehement opposition to the Vietnam War.

A spinoff was the Four-Letter-Word or Free Speech Movement. Mario Savio and his student followers asked that there be no restrictions on the content of speech or on academic freedoms, though eventually, he conceded that within those freedoms, there should be a sense of responsibility. The movement became a laughing stock to the general public, and diluted the importance of free speech issues and opposition to the war.

All this was in our newspapers, but it hardly affected Palo Alto and the Peninsula. Much closer to home, though, was the increased use of LSD, the hippie movement, and the radical Students for a Democratic Society (SDS). People high on LSD were having bad trips and running around town naked. Some friends and I, driving in Marin County, saw a naked young woman frantically running in and out of traffic. She appeared completely out of her mind. A wise counselor in our car jumped out and, to my naive surprise, seemed to know exactly what to do. She lovingly cared for the woman, a college student, and gently took her to a gas station restroom. We called the police, who drove the woman to a nearby hospital. We were shaken up to see first-hand the damage LSD could do.

San Francisco's Haight-Ashbury district became the center for this new drug culture. The earlier bohemians and the beat movement could no longer find reasonable lodging in the city's North Beach area, where they had been centered since the 1950s, and so were turning to relatively cheap Haight-Ashbury, near Golden Gate Park.

In spite of LSD incidents, an experimental institute to understand the drug's effects—and perhaps its benefits—was established in Menlo Park, the next town north of Palo Alto and Stanford University. It made hallucinogenic drugs available under controlled conditions, letting people pay for an LSD experience in an "ideal environment." Two psychologists or trained counselors were present, along with a sanctuary-like atmosphere; quiet, "spiritual" music; and low lighting. The LSD was taken from a jeweled chalice, like the Holy Grail. Jim, a friend from work, said when I meet him in the coffee shop at the back of Kepler's Books in Menlo Park: *John, you can't believe it! I have just had the greatest experience of my whole life! The $500 I had to pay was incredibly worth it, and I'm going to start saving up to do it again.*

I was fascinated, and asked for details. The experience was carefully designed. It was quite a ceremony, and nothing was rushed. Though the directors of the Menlo Park Institute tried to ensure that no one had a "bad trip," the truth became clear: The results of taking LSD were unpredictable and could lead to major problems. The institute closed after a few months. I never found out if Jim went back for his second trip.

Timothy Leary, a brilliant Harvard professor turned guru, gave a lecture at Berkeley extolling LSD. His mantra was "Turn on, tune in, drop out." When a student who heard him jumped to his death from the top story of a dorm two days later, some people connected the two events. Clearly these were not the old bohemians. Many teen-agers were running away from home and ending up in the Haight looking for a pad and a trip.

Eastern thought was becoming popular too. I still have my copy of *Be Here Now* by Baba Ram Dass (who was Richard Alpert when he taught at Harvard). The first chapter details his movement from academic success to the world of Eastern thought. I studied his book in great detail, and in many ways lived on the edge of that culture, although I never actually became part of it myself.

A good aspect of this movement was that young people were asking big questions: *Can I find purpose in life? What is its ultimate meaning? What is truth?* These are the questions every serious thinker must face. As a follower of Jesus, I was beginning to find an answer in terms of a God who loves us. For those of us who want to engage in such a conversation, there is nothing worse than indifference. Thus we were in our element at the Haight.

I asked myself: How viable are the Christian answers to the great existential questions of meaning, evil, and death? Did they make sense in the new Counterculture? I was part of a men's group from different Peninsula churches that established a rescue mission in the Haight. I drove up there with my friend Carl Gallivan, six feet, three inches tall with long hair and a big, friendly smile. There was no furniture in our mission front room, and we all sat cross-legged on a huge welcoming carpet. A sign outside read: *Welcome all! If you are looking for answers, we have some.* There was always coffee brewing and a warm welcome for drop-ins. Not surprisingly, there were plenty of them, many without a place to stay, runaway teen-agers from middle-class families looking for an alternative lifestyle. I was not sure how clear our reasoned words of hope were, but if our lives showed love and compassion, we believed we could make a difference. There was nothing as good as a safe place to sleep and a hot cup of soup. If we could get a home phone number and call the parents, we could be a link to sanity.

THE SDS AT STANFORD

Down on the San Francisco Peninsula, the SDS, the radical, left-wing group formed in 1965, was active at Stanford. In 1968, Francis and Edith Schaeffer from Switzerland were visiting us and were interested in relating to the counterculture. I took Dr. Schaeffer to the offices of the *Stanford Daily,* which had been taken over by SDS students. We found them promoting violent action against the establishment, the university, the Stanford Research Institute, Lockheed, and other organizations. Their prophets were the three M's: Marx, Mao, and Marcuse. Clearly this was far beyond protesting the war in Vietnam. Schaeffer asked: *How would you rearrange society?* The answer was very clear. *Society is so corrupt we want to tear it down and start again. Read Marcuse. It might mean we have to break it down into small city-states. Somehow a better system has to be found.*

How would this work? Schaeffer's questioning produced no good answers. As we left, I was surprised that he was undisturbed by their violent solutions and told them, *You are warmly invited to visit my home in Switzerland. It is a community which wrestles with these same questions.* I was impressed by his approach to the young people: It was simple: *The compassionate love of Christ and total vulnerability meets peoples' needs."* Later, in the '70s, when we was supervising a small community for young people, modeled after Switzerland, in the Santa Cruz Mountains, I visited the collection of chalets in the little village of Huemoz, Switzerland, that make up the L'Abri community. It had two aims: to give honest answers to honest questions and to provide a home for anyone in need. This was something we were trying to do in a small way at our Haight rescue mission.

LUNCH WITH BRUCE FRANKLIN

Two of my friends and I arranged to have lunch with Bruce Franklin, an associate professor of English at Stanford who was known as an outstanding Herman Melville scholar. Recently he had been suspended by the university president for provoking violence by radical students. Among other provocations, he told students who were considering damaging the Computer Center to, "Shut it down."The year was 1971, and the United States had just escalated the Vietnam war. I was sick at the news.

The big question for the Stanford administration was: Had Franklin gone beyond exercising his right to free speech by advocating an illegal act? What fascinated me and my friends were the questions: What is driving this man? What is his worldview? How do I communicate rationally with someone who has such controversial beliefs? How do I as a follower of Jesus relate to him?

We met in a cafe near the university. Here was Bruce, looking like any modestly dressed academic, without the long hair of many radicals. I was with Dr. Gerhardt Dirks, a brilliant inventor who had escaped from Germany by night after World War II with a suitcase full of original patents for electronic memory, one of the keys to the IBM disk drive. He understood communism from the inside. With us was my close friend, Al Fabrizio, an artist, designer, and musician. The conversation went nowhere. We found that Bruce was a strong advocate for Mao and the Cultural Revolution. Terrible stories were beginning to emerge of how millions were suffering. He declined to believe them. Gerhardt was inevitably agitated. He had a problem even listening to our dialog. I saw here a lesson about conflict: We cannot listen to each other if we are enemies.

The breakthrough came when we start talking about human relations and family values. Suddenly we were on common ground. Bruce shared about his son, and wondered how he should bring him up in today's world. We shared our own struggles. Sadly, Gerhardt was still frozen. It seemed he simply could not get over the huge ideological differences we had, understandably since he and his family had been so badly hurt by communism.

I was learning that in order to communicate well, I had to start on common ground. I was humbled by Bruce's total commitment to his cause, which clearly involved his whole family. How committed was I to a message of peace and reconciliation? In trying to understand Bruce's position. I reexamined my own. We all have blind spots. After a year of much discussion and debate, Bruce was dismissed from Stanford. I wish we could have stayed in touch.

Christmas with the Cleavers

Years later, in 1978, when I had a thriving family, we spent Christmas Day with the family of Eldridge Cleaver. He had become famous earlier as a prominent black radical, a leader of the Black Panther movement, and author of *Soul On Ice*, written in prison. The book had a profound effect on the black liberation movement. Cleaver had spent several years of exile in Cuba, Algeria, and France, financed by North Korea, before becoming a follower of Jesus. He had returned to the U.S. in 1975 and renounced violence, and was now living in Menlo Park.

My daughter Lisa was eight, and son Jonathan five. Bethany Lutheran, their elementary school, was where the two Cleaver children also attended. Alma, my wife, had been chatting with Kathleen Cleaver after school one day and found that her family had no plans for Christmas, so invited them over. The four children got on well with each other, and Kathleen was a gracious guest.

Her mother, lively and articulate, visiting from the East Coast, also joined us. After dinner, the children played outside on the grass. It was a pleasure seeing them enjoying their time together, but there was also a pang of sadness in knowing that our middle-class society in the Bay Area still had a serious racial divide.

Eldridge was completely at ease and very relaxed. The women did most of the talking. Kathleen was articulate and totally "with it." She was strikingly beautiful. It became clear that she and her family had gone through much turmoil but that she was triumphing over the past. Our conversation, though not mentioning the Black Panthers, covered a wide range of subjects. When we focused on the children, things got lively. We were on common ground. That was what really mattered, and the conversation flowed easily. Overall, we enjoyed their visit immensely and were enriched by it. We later heard that the family had moved back to Oakland, and we lost contact. Their visit was a perfect example of Alma's natural way of relating to others.

I now move from the color blue to indigo, from being a single thirty-five-year-old starting his own company in what will soon be Silicon Valley to marriage, home ownership, children, and all that they involve.

Chapter 6

Love, Marriage, and a Growing Family

Indigo is the color between primary blue and violet. It is also the name of my step great-granddaughter, symbolizing for me the love of our growing and extended family. Its wavelength range is 430 to 455 nanometers.

When Alma returned from Switzerland, I seemed to have forgotten her, as I was so involved with the Haight-Ashbury mission and trying to start my company. Many things were pressing on me, keeping the latent love out of sight. In 1966, I took the big step of leaving Hewlett-Packard. I set up the office of Spectrex, my one-man company, in my rented cottage in Palo Alto. The shop for assembling and aligning spectroscopes was in a nearby garage

As Spectrex started to grow, I found I needed a part-time secretary, and Alma offered to help. She had become the company nurse at Varian Associates, only five minutes' walk from my cottage, and came over after work to type out mailings to help sell the Vreeland spectroscope. When I dropped by her clinic at work to deliver a rush job she was going to type, I noticed how caring and gracious she was with the other employees. I also noticed that she was completely at ease with people. Her care and concern for others was inescapable.

If there were ever a sign from heaven, I knew I had one: I was still undecided about our relationship, but as I drove up El Camino Real, the main road through town, I saw her driving her

red Oldsmobile in the op-
posite direction and realized in a moment that I
truly loved her. It was as
clear as daylight. Her light
came flooding into my life.
I wondered why I had been
so slow to see her in her
scintillating beauty.

My love for Alma was no
ephemeral dream or wish-
ful thinking but was as real
as my heartbeat. Beyond
emotion, it became a door-

Alma in her nursing uniform.

way to a new and richly colored reality. I proposed and, wonder
of wonders, she accepted. The wedding was at our Palo Alto
church, where we had first met. Our much-loved pastor, Ray
Stedman, did the honors. He had a way of making a wedding
before a crowded assembly an intimate and holy occasion. We
settled into our new home in Menlo Park, the next town north
of Palo Alto, and did our best to develop a holistic, integrated
lifestyle. The particular brand of Christianity we were involved
in was not strict or legalistic. It was open, robust, and dynamic,
discovering new frontiers of faith in the environment and the
counterculture. It provided a bridge between the Jesus movement, the radical left, and middle-class Palo Alto. In the "body
life" services on Sunday evenings, needy folk were able to take
out of the collection plate as well as put into it.

Elisabeth Grace (Lisa) was born in January 1969, a year after
our wedding. The hospital had just begun letting fathers be present at delivery, so I felt privileged to be there to see our beautiful
baby girl take her first breath. The miracle of birth has never
ceased to amaze me. To actually hold this jewel in my arms and
see Alma's beaming face was a moment of great joy, a particular

kind of joy, participating with the woman I loved in a God-like function: the creation of a new and vibrant life. I counted Lisa's fingers and toes. Yes, there were ten of each. I handed her back to Alma, where she snuggled up to her mother's breast. At home that evening, I prepared for the new arrival—crib, diapers, changing table—and ensured that our home was warm enough. The next day, Alma and Lisa arrived, and the notion of being three distinct persons under one roof sank in.

When Lisa was just six months old, we took our first of several trips to Europe. In England, my parents were still running Dungate Manor as a guest house for the elderly. They refused to call themselves elderly even though my dad was eighty-four at the time. He would tell friends, "My wife and I run a home for the elderly" without the slightest hint of immodesty. He had taken a solo round-the-world trip two years earlier to visit our far-flung family in New Zealand and the U.S. After thirty-two years as a physician and surgeon in China, he refused to retire. He loved taking walks in the rolling Surrey countryside, and during our visit, he and I walked and talked as much as we could.

There was a lot of ground to cover, physically and emotionally. We discussed the physicality of getting old, the problems of running the Manor, the six thousand miles that separated us, and my brother Robin's schizophrenia. Of my siblings, only Elizabeth remained in England to give support for Robin and my parents in their old age. But something was nagging me; I didn't know what. Years later, I discovered that I still had not forgiven my father for leaving me and my siblings in that boarding school on the coast of China when he and our mother traveled inland in 1940. It would take another twenty-two years and some wise counseling before I could see how my lack of forgiveness had affected me. Even though he had passed away at the time, I wrote him a letter of forgiveness and love, with tears flowing, and a great burden was lifted.

In 1972, Jonathan was born, so now we were four. Our Menlo Park home was ideal for bringing up the two. The back yard had some huge oaks, a tree house, and a pool. Both children learned to swim at an early age. I have a Super 8 movie of Jonathan swimming across the pool at age two with a rubber doll in one hand. It did not seem to slow him down. (He later played on his high school water polo team.) We never lacked for baby-sitters, with all the single folks we knew in town and at the local L'Abri center. Our home became an open house for young people, mainly in their twenties. We were both in our thirties, so did not feel any significant age gap.

One of our favorite campsites was north of San Francisco, in Marin County. Samuel Taylor State Park nestles deep in old growth redwoods on the road to the coast. It was always an adventure: packing up the tent, sleeping bags, and cooking equipment; loading the Volvo station wagon; driving up through San Francisco and then across the Golden Gate Bridge. Often, there was summer fog flooding in from the ocean and an air of mystery when the magnificent views would suddenly disappear in the whiteness and then reappear. It was a dance of light. Then there were the favorite campsites. The best were in a circle of redwoods. We would lie on a sleeping bag, gazing up to a cathedral of unsurpassed beauty, and wade in the creek chasing crawfish.

Over the hill lay the ocean and Point Reyes. When Lisa was ten and Jonathan seven, while driving over to the lighthouse at Point Reyes, we were met by a total surprise: An Elizabethan galleon came sailing into the bay east of the point with all flags flying. It was a magnificent sight, so we headed toward the beach. What a coincidence, for we happened to have come across the four hundredth anniversary of Sir Francis Drake's landing on California soil and claiming it for the queen. We watched spellbound as a tender was launched from the ship with sailors in Elizabethan costume. They were greeted on shore by Indian natives. There was an exchange of gifts and a sense of general well-being. Drake's chaplain led a short service of thanks to Almighty God for their safe arrival. Our drive back to camp was filled with stories of Elizabethan history, the Armada, Drake, Sir Walter Raleigh, and their voyages of adventure. It also led to a family discussion on the history of California and the ownership of land. Being members of the Sierra Club and getting its monthly bulletins helped us all develop an appreciation for nature and our responsibility for protecting it.

Our home was a five-minute walk from Menlo-Atherton High School, so once Lisa and Jonathan started school there, they would often invite friends over for lunch. We parents then had the pleasure of getting to know the circle they were in socially. It didn't hurt that we installed a pickle ball court which was much used. After graduating, Lisa started college at the University of California in San Diego. We made a glorious trip of the drive there down the Big Sur coast. Jonathan was fifteen then, had a great circle of friends, and was involved in competitive swimming and water polo. He excelled at German and later became fluent in French and Italian as well.

In the summer of 1987, Alma had been experiencing recurring abdominal pain and was found to have an ovarian cyst. Suddenly, life became dark with apprehension and worry. The cyst was removed but contained cancer cells. Alma started chemotherapy, though we knew ovarian cancer was one of the hardest types to treat. She and I would lie awake in the dark wondering and praying for healing and peace. All sorts of questions raced through my head: "Could the tumor have been detected earlier?" "What is the possibility of a cure and full recovery?"

I started to look at Alma in a different way. She became more beautiful to me. I had always loved her hands, but now they took my breath away. The thought of her not recovering was a monster, living in the closet and coming out to haunt us on a regular basis. We wondered, "How does being followers of Jesus make a difference in our situation?" We found comfort in Psalm 23: *Though I walk through the valley of the shadow of death, I will fear no evil, for you are with me; your rod and your staff, they comfort me.*

As much as through Scripture, certain pieces of music invited us into a new oneness and courage. In particular, we loved Brahms' two sonatas for violin and piano; the two instruments are in intimate dialog. Though comforts like these could not tell us "why" we must face the possible coming of death, they helped us grasp some peace and a sense of God's love that reached beyond the uncertain future.

I was sitting by Alma's bed a few days before she passed away. We were holding hands and she said, "John, I want to tell you something. When I am gone, you will probably consider remarrying. I want you to know that you have my full blessing." I kissed her tenderly and was speechless. The thought was far from my mind, but she had thought it all through.

Her last twelve months were the darkest of our life together. It took seventeen months in all for the cancer to finally take her life. An article in *The New Yorker* described Emerson's loss of his five-year-old son, who died of scarlet fever. Emerson's grief was intense, and yet he wrote in a letter the following week, "I chiefly grieve that I cannot grieve." His actual experience of grieving did not seem real to him, or real enough for the great loss that had overwhelmed his life. I experienced a similar overwhelming response when Alma passed away after our twenty-one years of marriage.

My grieving seemed unworthy of the enormity of the loss. Grief was a cruel visitor to our home. The loss was like a permanent wound, or dangerously like an amputation. I seemed completely cut off from the life we had made together. I wanted to grieve more, to make it more worthy of Alma, but nothing I could do adequately honored her precious life. As a survivor, I knew, I must press on and live a full and generous life in spite of such a loss.

Lisa put her sophomore year on hold and moved back home from college for a semester. She and Jonathan, who was in his senior year of high school, became my strength and purpose for living. At this crucial time, I realized my children were my priceless treasures. The light of my life had gone out, but I could see that light in the faces of my children as we moved into the future together.

Poetry, Art, and a New Life

*Violet is the color at the far end of the visible spectrum. It is what we might
see just after the sun sets. Its wavelength range is 380 to 430 nanometers.*

For several months, I was in shock at the loss of my love,
my life partner, and the mother of our two children. I
continued to put my energies into Spectrex. Perhaps that,
and Lisa and Jonathan's closeness and patience with me, are
what saved me from depression. I was grateful for the challenge
of day-to-day engineering. We continued our monthly L'Abri
discussion evenings with their cultural and spiritual dynamic
but sorely missed Alma and her warm hospitality.

Emily Dickinson wrote: "Not knowing when the dawn will
come, I open every door."She was waiting for the light, long before
it came. She was ready for it, with all the doors open, let alone the
windows. After a year, there was the hint of a dawn for me. I realized how miserable life can be in singleness after such a happy
marriage. A few months later, I was ready to begin thinking afresh
about companionship. Tom and Karen Cooper, close friends in
Vancouver, B.C., wrote and mentioned a friend of theirs, Luci
Shaw, whom they thought I might like to meet. I pricked up my
ears. She was a poet, which interested me, as poetry was an important part of family life in England. Then the Coopers sent me
a thick, hardcover book, *God in the Dark*. Luci was the author. The
book was perfect for me. On the back cover was a comment by
writer and theologian Frederick Buechner: "Luci Shaw pulls no
punches and proposes no simplistic answers in this eloquent ac-

count of her husband's death. With the eye of a poet and a searching faith, she has written a very honest and haunting book."

I realized Luci must have gone through a similar grief to mine. I devoured the book, and wished I could meet her. My answers to grief and loss seemed trite compared with hers. She came through the ordeal of suffering with and for her husband, Harold, dying of lung cancer, with the kind of questioning faith that is at once deep, robust, and realistic. I hungered for that faith, and had a taste of it from reading her eloquent memoir.

The Coopers arranged a blind date in Vancouver. Luci flew in from her home in Wheaton, Illinois. I flew up from California. The four of us met at a downtown Greek restaurant, and I looked across the table at Luci's smiling face. For me, there was simply the pleasure of meeting someone with such writing skills and honesty while facing death. That was all I wanted or needed then, but something deeper must have been awakening. She was lovely.

We spent much of that weekend together, and discovered common ground. Both of us had medical missionary parents; hers served in the Solomon Islands and mine in China. I told her of my love for poetry, and found that she had published seven books of poems. Both of us had lost our spouses through cancer. I shared what her book, *God in the Dark*, meant to me. We found we both have a love of adventure. During a later trip to New Zealand, she bungee-jumped while I watched in amazement. Most important, we found that we are on similar spiritual journeys. To our mutual joy, we found that we both liked Marmite, a dark, murky English spread—perfect on hot buttered toast.

I returned to California and tried to forget Luci, who was off on an overseas publishing trip. On her return, I called: "Luci, may I fly out and visit you?" There were no objections that I could detect but instead a gentle, questioning "Yes." When I arrived, she was baking cookies. I had not been there very long and we were standing on the balcony looking at a full moon. There, on the spot, I proposed to her and, amazingly, she accepted my offer of marriage. Her reply told me that the love we had discovered for each other was real. Humanly speaking, this quick romance was inexplicable. It was only the second time we had met. Lisa and Jonathan had never met her and had hardly heard of her. Somehow, though, we knew this was the real thing. As we talked, her cookies were burned to a frazzle.

I flew back to Menlo Park and tried to explain my love for Luci to Lisa and Jonathan, but it was not easy for them, as their mother had passed away less than a year and a half earlier. I certainly must have seemed impetuous, but, looking back twenty-eight years, it was right. Wisely, Luci and I postponed our wedding until the new year to help both families adjust and get to know each other.

So began my life with Luci. This was a new kind of love for me: wonderful, fresh, and alive, and we were young again. In fact, we were to find a deep, mature beginning to a life commitment. I was fifty-nine, and she had just turned sixty-three. I was reminded that my own dad was fifty-nine at his second marriage. Lisa was still studying at the University of California in San Diego, while Jonathan, then eighteen, was in his first year at Stanford.

One memorable evening, we all were sailing up San Francisco Bay from Redwood City to a planned overnight berth at Coyote Point, nearer San Francisco. A sunset glow softened the shadows of San Bruno Mountain to our west. Five of us were on the cruise, as Luci's son John and Lisa and Jonathan had come along. Luci went alone to stand at the bow. It was a special moment for her; a few days later, she wrote this poem:

Sailing San Francisco Bay

She braces—one hand
on the forestay. The other hand
curved around to the outside of the jib,
its belly heavy with wind.

Pressing against her hand heel,
deceptive as silk, the air
fills the sailcloth until it bulks
as pregnant as her own body
before the last birth. Out there
on the Catalina's prow, with
the small waves swelling against
the hull under her so that
through the soles of her deck shoes
she feels the waters breaking,
she is alone, letting it all go
with the water sliding away below.
The other sounds—curlew cries across
the water, Mozart on the portable player,
the glasses and voices from the cabin —
all trail behind, like the faint call of her
grown children, gone in the green wake.

It is all such old magic—bitter sweet
like birth, the melting sea silver,
stained sky red, vanishing between
her legs like the last light being sucked
down through the bones of the mountains,
there in a bloody show.
She flattens her hand and pushes hard
against the blue cloth so that the sail
spills some of its wind,
giving it back to the bay.

Later, she asked herself what was behind it. Her conclusion was that she was releasing her children, letting them go on with their own lives, as she considered this new life with a new husband in a new place. We fixed the wedding date and were married in January 1991, with all seven children involved, her five

John and Luci.

and my two. Our honeymoon was a week of little miracles, discovering more about each other.

Several years later, we decided to move from California to Bellingham, Washington, halfway between Seattle and Vancouver, B.C., where Luci already had a small home. It is wonderful being married to a poet, as—any day of the week and any time of day—I can look over her shoulder at her computer screen and there, before my eyes, would be the jewel of a newborn poem.

In 2014, I sold Spectrex to its employees, fifty years after starting it in my little cottage. I had great peace of mind knowing it was in the good hands of Steve, Loan, and Liz. This meant less traveling down to the Bay Area, but I am constantly drawn south by the fact that Lisa and her family live there. She, Ben, and their two daughters, Rachel and Nicki, live in Palo Alto and are a source of constant joy, especially when I visit. I see in Lisa the gift of hospitality that she inherited from Alma. The dining room table is expandable and can easily and often does seat twelve. There is always something exciting going on when I visit: Rachel, in high school, with a track meet perhaps, or Nicki, in middle school, with volleyball. Ben is a psychologist with the San Mateo School District. Lisa works at Stanford Hospital as a nurse practitioner specializing in pediatric immunology. Jeff, one

Left: Lisa, Nicki, Rachel, and Ben. Right: Martina, Jonathan, and Alma.

of Luci's sons, and his family also live in the Bay Area, so Luci often joins me on these trips. Flying is the quick option, but our joy is to drive through the redwoods and along the magnificent coastal road.

Trips to visit Jonathan are inevitably less frequent, as he lives in Italy. After graduating from Stanford, he moved to Italy to pursue a career in art restoration. Today, he is a conservator of artistic and architectural works, and lives and works in Venice. He and Martina have a beautiful young daughter, Alma, named after her grandmother. His specialty is the restoration of stone, and his website shows his work on two Renaissance statutes of Adam and Eve in the Doge's palace.

Every four or five years, Lisa, Jonathan, and I, along with Richard Jolly, organize a "Hannibal Reunion Hike." We invite friends and family to join us at Hannibal's pass, the Col de Clapier, during the summer. There, we celebrate Hannibal's crossing in 218 B.C. and Jumbo's crossing in 1959, and read Hannibal's famous speech encouraging his exhausted troops. We are usually forty or fifty hikers, and we end the day with a banquet with awards, speeches, and songs.

This leads to my next project: I am defending the Col de Clapier as Hannibal's pass from a new and, we believe, unfounded theory proposing a more-southern pass. Dr. Bill Mahaney, a Canadian geomorphologist, discovered a massive pattern of ancient manure near the Col de la Traversette in the southern Alps, and conjectured, "Could this be elephant dung?" His question hit the headlines in the summer of 2017 with an extensive article in *The Smithsonian*.

Richard and I climbed to the Col de la Traversette in 1956, and to us, it clearly did not fit Polybius's description of Hannibal's pass. Moreover, the dung could have been accumulated over centuries from pack horses and mules. Mahaney's research team has isolated five ascaris eggs from the manure. Genome sequencing may be able to tell the type of animals that left the droppings, and perhaps their geographic origin. While awaiting possibly definitive results, I have invited Mahaney to open debate, possibly on Canadian TV, and suggested that he and/or his defenders join our next climb to the Col de Clapier. The question of Hannibal's route has been researched for hundreds of years. I am not surprised that it is still alive and well.

Bellingham is a good place in which to retire: a town on the edge of Puget Sound, with the San Juan Islands to the west and the Cascade Range to the east, sandwiched between two different kinds of beauty. Luci and I love to camp, especially in a campground on the Nooksack River, on the way to Mount Baker. While Luci is working on another book of poems, I am happily sketching, landscape painting, or learning a new piece on the guitar. I exhibit my pen-and-ink drawings and paintings at Village Books, our local independent bookstore, and at other venues.

Every Wednesday, I spend time at a local elementary school with a nine-year-old boy who has family problems and does not relate well to others. We enjoy water color painting together, and I am gaining his confidence. This brings me full circle to when I was his age and Mom and Dad left me at the boarding school in China. A teacher there took me under her wing and encouraged me to draw. That made all the difference, and I am glad to return the favor seventy-six years later.

Luci and I are now in our eighties. We find pleasure in stopping to watch the daily sunsets, often lovely even in stormy weather. I return to my theme of light. After the darkness of the Japanese internment camp, there was the light of my new life in England. After the dark loss of Alma, there is the light of my new life with Luci and with Jonathan and Lisa and their families.

One of Luci's books of poetry is titled *What the Light Was Like*. Years ago, she and a poet friend would send each other postcards. The challenge was to describe what the light was like wherever they happened to be. I have shared with you what the light in my life has been like in its persistence. Its beauty and colors are everywhere. To the people of China, land of my birth, the color violet, at the end of the rainbow, represents the harmony of the universe.

My Parents' Journey through No-Man's-Land

The only thing you can take with you when you get to heaven is what you have given away.

—C.S. Lewis

The story that gripped me most, as told by dad on the troopship to England, was of my parents' three-month journey over fifteen hundred miles from the coast to far-off Lanchow in 1940. Mom and Dad had to cross the no-man's-land between the Japanese army and Chinese Nationalist troops, with ever-unexpected Communist guerillas complicating the journey.

Then there was the problem of the Yellow River, which had overflowed its banks that summer, pouring out enormous floods over vast areas of the flat countryside. Mom and dad had to cross it in four places, the first over twenty miles wide. One wonders why they ever set out in the first place. Perhaps they did not know how extensive the floods were or how dangerous the fighting was. After prolonged bartering to get a reasonable price, the four missionaries and their fourteen handcarts carrying fourteen hundred pounds of luggage were loaded onto flat-bottomed punts. The heavy boxes were placed at the bottom, and on top of them were balanced the handcarts. The humans squeezed themselves into cracks or perched themselves wherever they could. They were so crowded that it was a tight fit even to sit down. Mom was the only woman in the party, and she seemed to have taken things in stride, sketching along the way. Motive power was provided by coolies who wielded long poles to punt them along, or else they used crude oars made of a piece of rough board nailed onto the end of a short pole.

And so they set off. There was no skipper. Each man punted as hard as he could in whichever direction seemed most convenient without much regard to the course to be steered. Naturally, this turned out to be most erratic. After a full day of punting, they were still far from the other side. This continued into the night, and soon after 4 a.m., the boats got into a good flow running in the right direction which carried them along at a fine pace—until there was a terrific bump. The boat suddenly stopped, and the boatman in front was thrown into the water. They had hit a submerged stump, which stove in one of the stout planks at the bottom of the hull. Instantly, they heard the loud rush of water pouring in. Fortunately, they were close to a village just beyond the water. Hastily, the boatmen hauled the craft to it and unloaded all the freight. Carts, trunks, boxes, bedding, rucksacks, food basket, gramophone, records, typewriter, and the missionaries were dumped unceremoniously onto this mud pile. Soon after daylight, rescue came in the form of two boats, and they were able to set off once more across the swirling brown waters. In a few hours, they had reached the other side.

Land travel was slow, with the carts pushed by coolies at an average of two and a half miles an hour. Mom rode along the bumpy tracks in a small handcart, made as comfortable as possible with rolls of bedding. She considered herself "guardian of the goods," and always made her cart last of the fourteen. And so they traveled on, stopping at little villages for brief rest. The inns of Henan Province were the worst they had ever seen. The rooms had mud walls and thatched roofs, no doors, and no paper in the windows. The courtyards were dirty beyond description. The travelers preferred threshing floors for the night.

The party was fired on three times by soldiers and narrowly missed being hit. One guerrilla chief refused to allow them to proceed through his territory for several days. During their enforced wait, Dad began treating some of the soldiers for minor ailments. Among them was the chief cook, who had a badly ulcerated leg. Afterward, the cook put in a word for them, and a few hours later, boats appeared to take them on the next part of the journey.

They were almost through to the next mission station and were spending the night in another guerrilla encampment when two strange, well-roped bundles among their luggage aroused Dad's suspicions. When asked what the contents were, the coolies were silent. Dad insisted that the bundles be opened. Inside were forty-eight packets of heroin. To be caught with such a drug would mean immediate imprisonment and possibly death. Dad insisted that the bundles be removed at once. One very frightened coolie stammered, *Those do not belong to us. They belong to Mr. Lee,* a plump Chinese merchant who had been tagging along with their party for a few days. Mr. Lee was away until that evening, and the coolie promised to get him to remove the drugs. Next morning, he assured Dad that the drugs had been disposed of. As there was no sign of Mr. Lee, Dad insisted on a search of the luggage. Sure enough, one by one, all forty-eight packets of heroin were found hidden in the bedding rolls or among the cooking utensils.

Just then, a soldier stepped through the courtyard gates and said his chief had given them permission to leave, after several days' delay, but it had to be immediately. This was indeed a crisis. If the packets were left behind, they would be discovered and ownership traced to the mission party. With pressure from the guard, the coolies began to move out with all the boxes on their wheelbarrows. Miraculously, when only three carts were left, Mr. Lee appeared. The heroin was forced unceremoniously into his hands, and the party went on its way, leaving him standing alone in the empty courtyard with the incriminating goods in his possession. As we kids heard this fascinating story, we all wondered what had happened to Mr. Lee?

After that delay, there was another two-week holdup getting into *free China*, which was controlled by the Nationalist army. It was late November by then, with the weather getting colder, and they had more mountains to cross before reaching Lanchow. Finally, over three months after leaving us on the coast, they arrived at their destination.

APPENDIX B

Jumbo and Her Family: A Case for Our Love and Their Survival

Team members of the 1959 British Alpine Hannibal Expedition developed great affection for Jumbo, our traveling companion. By the end of the trip, we were convinced of her vibrant personality and team spirit. Instead of viewing her as a circus attraction and we her keepers, she kept on indicating, in the ways she enjoyed herself and responded to our affection, that she was her own keeper and team member. She was truly "one of us." There was in her demeanor a spirit of adventure that we as a team appreciated. We all experienced a sad and emotional parting when we had to say good-bye to her at the end of our expedition.

From a wider perspective, Jumbo represented her whole family. This unique species, these mighty elephants, both Indian and African, stretch across Southeast Asia to Africa. Here she was, representing her kind, on an adventure with a human team, behaving very much like those humans, as we all crossed the challenging Alpine terrain together, enjoying it to the hilt.

Humans and elephants, particularly the Indian ones, have worked together for centuries. We believe that a breed of African elephant, two thousand years ago, was roaming the lush Atlas Mountains of northwest Africa and domesticated by the Carthaginians. Yet today African elephants are considered untamable and generally unpredictable. Where has the magic gone?

We often like to attribute human characteristics to animals we love, particularly to cats, dogs and horses. They are our companions and our friends. We love them with a special, unique love that is similar to but different from love for fellow humans. They fulfill a particular need in our lives. In fact, these priceless creatures are a wonderful gift. Rudyard Kipling wrote movingly about the grief he went through after the death of his favorite dog. I still keep the collar of our golden retriever, Bungee, in my car. He died more than twenty years ago, but he meant so much to my family that his memory is as a healing balm.

How does the elephant fit into our spectrum of love and affection for animals? We love elephants, not that we can bring them into our homes, but because of who they are, the largest land animal in the world, both majestic and endearing. I am convinced that mankind has a unique and universal love for elephants. Recently, two elephants in the Seattle Zoo were to be shipped to a Midwestern zoo. A public outcry reflected the general opinion that they should not be "cooped up in a zoo" (although one had been their long-time home) but sent to an elephant sanctuary instead. What was it about those two pachyderms that pulled at the heartstrings of the people of Seattle?

Peter Matthiessen in *The Tree Where Man Was Born* wrote of elephants: "There is a mystery behind that masked, grey visage, an ancient life force, delicate and mighty, awesome and enchanted, commanding the silence reserved for mountain peaks, great fires and the sea."

Indian elephants have bonded with their mahouts for generations. They can relate to humans in a unique way. In India, an elephant and his mahout can be born on the same day, live a life of working together, and die on the same day. Their life span is the same.

Elephants are very social animals. Their social balance as a family or clan is unmatched by that of other mammals. "What is special about elephants is just how similar they are to us—socially and developmentally," says Caitlin O'Connell-Rodwell, a Stanford University ecologist. "If you watch a family group reuniting, their behavior is exactly like ours—the little cousins darting off together, and the elaborate greetings of adults. Elephants offer a way of us looking into a mirror, for better or worse."

There might have been a strong case for bringing two elephants on our trip, as they love companionship. We considered it, but clearly Signor Terni had only one elephant available, and we were running on a tight budget. Jumbo would have enjoyed an elephant companion, but it did not seem necessary as her relationship with Ernesto was strong and endearing. In a very real sense, their relationship was the basis for the expedition's success.

To further illustrate the huge affection humans have for elephants, all we have to do is look at children's literature. Babar the Elephant has earned a special place as a hero in nursery literature, and he and the depictions in several *Babar* books are in a class by themselves. The illustrations by Jean de Brunhoff are superb. Then, of course, there is A. A. Milne's *Heffalump*, though he is just a dream animal that Piglet and Winnie-the-Pooh plan to capture. Ernest Shepard's illustrations are delightful. I have been told that the line was so long to have a ride on *Dumbo,* the flying elephant, at Orlando's Magic Kingdom, that Disney had to make an exact copy of the ride to cut waiting times in half.

Rudyard Kipling had affection for elephants and wrote about them for children. "The Elephant's Child," otherwise known as "How the Elephant Got Its Trunk," is as good a children's story as one can find, and the wonder over the elephant's trunk that many of us experienced when young is graphically enhanced. For older children, the stories in *The Jungle Book* are pure magic. I remember, as a twelve-year-old reading a tattered copy from the Weihsien camp library, being enchanted by the story "Toomai of the Elephants." Kala Nag, the great one, is devoted to Toomai, the son of his mahout. He takes Toomai on his back to show him the elephants' dance in the heart of the jungle at midnight. Perhaps that is where I first caught the magic of elephants.

It is true that elephants have a remarkable memory. There are many stories illustrating this. Living with Jumbo at the Turin Zoo,

Ernesto clearly saw instances of her good memory. When he took her out exercising in the hills above the city to train for the expedition, she quickly remembered the best routes to take and when and where she might expect a drink. Jumbo also developed strong affection or dislike for various members of the press who traveled with her. There was one reporter whom she disliked intensely, though we could never discover why. We acknowledged her sixth sense.

On a more serious note, African elephants are being decimated for their ivory tusks. In 1855, while sailing down the Zambezi River, David Livingstone, the famous missionary and explorer, came across an important chief's grave. On it were seventy huge tusks planted upright with their tips pointing inwards. Ten years later, the big game hunter Charles Baldwin followed Livingstone's trail and reported not a single tusk there. The terrible ivory trade had started. The irony is that the tusks, designed as a weapon to protect and thus to preserve the species, were to cause mass extermination of African elephants by humans.

In 1900, there were approximately 2 million African elephants in the wild. As of 2017, there were fewer than five hundred thousand. Central Africa lost 65 percent of its elephants in the last twenty years, most of them killed by poachers who then smuggled the ivory to Asia. China's growing economy and its insatiable desire for ivory has added to the problem.

The decimation of Asian elephants is not quite so serious, but from a population of over a hundred thousand last century, there are now fewer than fifty thousand now. The main reason is loss of habitat as the human populations of India, Thailand, and Indonesia increase and more land is placed under cultivation. However, the ivory trade is also a factor.

If you love elephants as I do, I suggest that you contribute to the World Wildlife Fund (www.wwf.org) in its efforts to preserve remaining elephant populations. Founded in 1961, the fund has done magnificent work with endangered species. On its website, you can adopt African elephants as your choice of where your money will go.

About the Author

As one of six children of British medical missionaries in China, John Hoyte grew up in a life built on family and faith. During World War II, he and his siblings, separated from their parents, were interned for nearly four years by the Japanese military. Grit, determination, and imagination were the only way to survive—and these became the basis for the next seven decades. John's amazing exploits included leading an elephant over the Alps to follow Hannibal's tracks and perfecting an invention that launched a fifty-year career in Silicon Valley.

His earlier book, *Alpine Elephant,* is now available as an ebook and as a paperback through Amazon. He created the whimsical sketches and maps in both *Alpine Elephant* and *Persistence of Light*.

John lives in Bellingham, Washington, with his wife, the poet Luci Shaw. His hobbies are sailing, pen-and-ink sketching, landscape painting, and playing classical guitar.

His website is www.johnhoyte.com. Follow him on Twitter @johnhoyte1 and on Facebook.